Praise for *Establishing Home*

Great design goes beyond just a pretty space and invites us into something bigger. What I love about *Establishing Home* is Jean's ability to create spaces that are equal parts function, beauty, and intuition. She'll inspire you in ways that help you design a home you love, with an approach that leaves room for the unexpected too. Home is so much more than the sum of its parts, and this beautiful book will encourage you to keep pursuing that which fills the gaps.

JOANNA GAINES
Cofounder of Magnolia

In *Establishing Home*, Jean Stoffer blesses us with her vast wisdom on everything from growing a business to raising a family to nurturing good design. With a career that has seen incredible longevity, Jean goes from mentor to mom and back in this book, generously bestowing us with advice on both life and design. You get the feeling, reading this book, that she believes in you and that the sense of home she so effortlessly creates is possible for all of us. She empowers us to "choose fine things" for our homes, and Jean is the finest of them all.

JULIA MARCUM
Chris Loves Julia

Bringing attention not only to her design aesthetic but also to her family dynamic and business acumen, Jean Stoffer shows us how to live and be beautiful. And I am here for it!

JACKIE HILL PERRY
Writer, speaker, and author of Holier Than Thou

Establishing Home

ESTABLISHING
—HOME—

*Creating Space for
a Beautiful Life with
Family, Faith, and Friends*

JEAN STOFFER

with September Vaudrey

TYNDALE
REFRESH™

Think Well. Live Well. Be Well.

Visit Tyndale online at tyndale.com.

Visit the author online at jeanstofferdesign.com.

Tyndale and Tyndale's quill logo are registered trademarks of Tyndale House Ministries. *Tyndale Refresh* and the Tyndale Refresh logo are trademarks of Tyndale House Ministries. Tyndale Refresh is a nonfiction imprint of Tyndale House Publishers, Carol Stream, Illinois.

Establishing Home: Creating Space for a Beautiful Life with Family, Faith, and Friends

Designed by Libby Dykstra

Edited by Stephanie Rische

For information about special discounts for bulk purchases, please contact Tyndale House Publishers at csresponse@tyndale.com, or call 1-855-277-9400.

Library of Congress Cataloging-in-Publication Data

A catalog record for this book is available from the Library of Congress.

ISBN 978-1-4964-6041-7

Printed in China

28 27 26 25 24 23 22
7   6   5   4   3   2   1

I dedicate this book to my dad, Donald Tittle (1932–2022),
who was the closest representation of the Father's love I could imagine.
His joy, optimism, and love for people inspired and blessed me.
His love for God was real and felt by me and many others.
He would have loved reading this story, as he influenced much of it.

Contents

*Every home
and every life
can become
even more
beautiful.*

Chapter 1

SUN & SAND

Fifteen minutes into our morning walk on the last day of our Sanibel Island vacation, Dale turned to me. "I'm D-U-N done," he said.

I looked at him, curious. "Is there something in particular you are referring to?" I asked.

"I'm done with my job. I'm not going back to the markets," he said. "It's time to leave that life behind. When we get home, I'm selling my seat on the exchange. It's too fast paced, too all-or-nothing. It's a young man's game, and I'm done."

I stopped in my tracks. "What? But—but you *are* a young man. You're only twenty-seven!" I countered. "You're so good at trading, and it's good money."

Dale was a commodities broker and trader at the Chicago Mercantile Exchange—and he was successful. His income provided significant financial stability for us as a newly married couple.

"I know, Jean. But every morning when I step out onto the trading floor, I feel like I might lose everything," he said. "That's not a good state of mind for this business. I might as well get out now before something bad happens. Then I can figure out what to do next."

I was stunned. "You're serious?"

"I'm serious. I'm done."

"And how long has this thought been in your head?" I asked. "I can't believe there's no discussion here. I know commodities has never been your long-term plan, but can't we talk this over?"

"Well, we're talking it over now."

"After you've already decided?"

"Yes. After I've already decided."

The thing about Dale is this: he is patient and easygoing, but when he decides on something, that's it. It's D-U-N. Done.

I wish I could say I tried to understand this decision from his point of view, but all I could think about was how it would affect my tidy life. We were financially dependent on Dale's earnings, and this announcement certainly wasn't what I was expecting on the last day of our vacation.

"I have decent money in my trading account, and I don't want to lose it," he said.

"Not a ton of money," I said. "We spent a good chunk of it on the apartment building." In the two years since getting married, we'd spent only a fraction of what he'd earned, but we'd spent some of our savings on an investment property.

"Yes, but it's enough to see us through until I figure out what's next. And we have your job . . ."

"My *minimum-wage* job," I retorted.

Looking back, I should have seen this coming. Deep down, both of us had always known Dale's commodities gig wouldn't last forever. He had watched too many colleagues blow out on the trading floor, losing everything and then some in a single day. He often talked about what the trading lifestyle did to some people who coped with the stress through alcohol, drugs, or lavish spending. He wanted nothing to do with that world, but it surrounded him day after day on the floor.

All these were signs I could have investigated—should have investigated—but didn't. I'd been busy enjoying our comfortable income and my part-time work. Dale's job had made a lot of things possible for us. We'd bought a town house and were remodeling it. We'd copurchased the apartment building and were remodeling it, too. Except for our first few months of marriage, we had never really struggled to make ends meet. I now realized those days were probably over.

As we resumed our walk along that Florida beach, I glanced over at Dale. He looked at peace, settled. *He's such a good man,* I thought. *True, I wish he had included me in this process so I could be fully on board by the time the decision was made, but I probably could have been more perceptive about how hard this has been on him.*

Our marriage was less than two years old, but it was solid. Dale was the kind of man who would never ask me to stay in a job I hated, nor could I bring myself to ask him to stay in a career he desperately wanted to leave.

I reached for his hand. "I'm mad at you, but we'll figure this out," I said. "We're in this together."

He squeezed my hand and exhaled.

Our flight home that afternoon was quiet, but my mind raced. Here was my new reality: I would be the sole breadwinner while Dale figured out what was next. I no longer had the luxury of working as an office manager in an interior-design firm—a field that fascinated me, even if the pay wasn't great. I needed to either find a job that paid more money or add a second job. *Doing what?*

Just seven days ago, our lives had been orderly and predictable. Now everything was up in the air. I needed to figure out what to do next.

As the world slipped by beneath our jet, I closed my eyes and prayed. *Lord, I'm angry and I'm scared. I don't like not knowing how this is going to turn out. I feel a huge sense of responsibility for this next season. Show me what you want me to do.*

GRAPH PAPER AND FINE THINGS

Growing up in the Midwest in the 1960s and 1970s, I was a typical twelve-year-old kid. I was the daughter of loving parents—the middle of three sisters who equally adored our baby brother. I excelled in sports and was decent at school, okay at music, and only mediocre at art.

Yet there I sat in Ms. Hall's sixth-grade art class, riveted.

"This project has two phases," our teacher explained. "First, you'll design the floor plan of a house." She turned on an overhead projector and placed a transparency on its glass surface. (It was the 1970s and PowerPoint was years away.) An architect's rendering of a simple, four-room plan appeared on the screen.

I'd never seen a floor plan before, but I loved its orderly, clean look. Architectural symbols showed me where the bathroom and kitchen were located. The windows, doors, closets, and a fireplace were all drawn to scale. It was like looking down at an empty home with its roof removed.

"Once I've approved your floor plan," Ms. Hall continued, "you'll use balsa wood and glue to build a 3D model of your house. Then you can decorate it, like this." She stooped behind her desk and lifted a tiny white house with green trim, mounted on a thin, square board.

I was mesmerized. *Now this is an art project I could get into!*

Ms. Hall passed around graph paper. "Take several sheets each," she said. "Use a pencil and a ruler to draw your floor plans over the weekend, and bring them in on Monday. And remember, your eraser is your friend."

Look for fine pieces, things that are classic, not trendy. Something fine will last.

After school I headed straight to my bedroom and pulled out a sheet of my graph paper. I drew a two-story house with three bedrooms and a bath upstairs and four rooms on the main floor. I labeled each of the rooms in capital letters, just as Ms. Hall had done: Bedroom 1, Bedroom 2, Bedroom 3, and Bath for the second floor; Living Room, Kitchen, and Dining Room for the first floor. But what would the other front room be? Another bedroom?

In the house we'd lived in when I was younger, my dad had a den. He did paperwork there, and sometimes he invited me in. That's where he taught me to play chess, and I had sweet memories in that room. On the fourth room of my floor plan, I wrote D-E-N.

Ms. Hall approved my floor plan on the first pass. I spent the next week constructing the 3D model of my little house, and I earned an A on the project. This was pretty much the extent of my artistic explorations during my growing-up years. We weren't an artsy family, but ours was a happy home. My

First day of school with my sisters, 1970—and me in a Lacoste dress from Grandpa Bradbury.

parents were good, solid people whose decisions were driven by practicality and Midwest frugality. Buying trendy new clothes or furniture to replace pieces that were perfectly functional—albeit outdated—would have never crossed their minds. We kids were never left wanting, though we may not have been setting any fashion trends at school either.

Me and Grandpa, 1965. Grandpa taught me from an early age that quality matters.

Except around Christmas. Each December, Grandpa Bradbury (my mom's dad) would take us kids on a special outing—a shopping trip with one grandchild at a time. On these trips, he would buy each of us a new Christmas outfit.

I loved those trips with Grandpa. He would pick me up in his Cadillac, always dressed to the nines in a tailored wool suit, Florsheim leather shoes, a topcoat, and a hat, and smelling faintly of pipe tobacco. He'd take me to lunch somewhere fancy, and then it was time for shopping.

"Quality matters," he told me as we wandered the children's department in the Marshall Field's flagship store on Chicago's State Street. "Look for fine pieces, things that are classic, not trendy. Something fine will last."

Most young teens my age would have rolled their eyes at the idea of their grandfather helping them shop for clothes, but my sisters and I knew better. Grandpa's taste was impeccable. He had an innate sense of fashion.

Back then, I didn't think of Grandpa Bradbury as an artist, but I can see now that he was. He didn't paint or draw or play an instrument. Instead, he filled his home with works of art, sculptures, and fine furniture, and he filled his closet with classic styles—fine wool suits, starched white shirts, and silk ties.

Although my mother wasn't as interested in the pursuit of fine things, Grandpa must have passed down his appreciation of art. She was an undeveloped artist—and quite talented. While studying elementary education at Northwestern University, she'd filled countless sketchbooks with her drawings.

When I was in high school, I came across those sketchbooks in her closet.

I was utterly surprised. "Mom, I had no idea you could draw!" I said. "These are really good! Why didn't you pursue your art?"

"Oh, honey," she said. "I got married right after college graduation and had your sister nine months later. I didn't have time to pursue my art as a young mom. I was quite happy to set that aside and focus on my family."

And focus she did. She was a remarkable mom to us kids. As I look back on the landscape of my childhood, what stands out about my mom is her constancy. She was consistently home when we were home, which gave us a sense of safety, peace, and order. On school days when my sisters and I walked home for lunch, my mom's smiling face greeted us as we stepped through the door, and a homemade lunch awaited us on the kitchen table.

My parents instilled in us practical skills that we'd need to become successful adults. Dad taught us how to do yard work and sparked our interest in sports, especially tennis. Mom encouraged us to babysit so we could earn our own money. She taught us how to change sheets on a bed, sort the laundry, and properly clean a house.

My favorite lesson was learning how to grocery shop with a well-planned list. I would ride my bike to the store and buy everything Mom needed. It may not sound like much, but when I was a kid, it made me feel so capable. I learned I could succeed at things I'd never done before. My mom's confidence in me gave me confidence in myself.

It's my mom I thank for the solid spiritual grounding I received as a child. When I was four, she became a Christian after reading Billy Graham's book *Peace with God*. She understood God's love for her in a powerful way, and it shaped the rest of her life. She read to us from the Bible and explained each passage in a way kids could understand. She read all seven of C. S. Lewis's Chronicles of Narnia books aloud at bedtime and explained the spiritual meaning behind the stories. Mom was so enthusiastic about her faith that it was contagious. She was (and still is) intentional, dedicated, and strong. Dad, too, followed Christ, and faith became the undergirding of our home.

My mom's confidence in me gave me confidence in myself.

Because of my parents' spiritual influence and example, I began a relationship with God myself. For as long as I can remember, I felt loved by him. I made my commitment to Christ official during a fourth-grade Sunday school class. The teacher asked if anyone would like to make a commitment that day, and I said I did. I felt close to him and didn't see any reason to put it off.

"I decided to follow Jesus and became a Christian today," I told my mom after church.

She hugged me. "That's a decision you'll never regret," she said. And she was right.

When I was eighteen, Mom developed cervical dystonia, an incurable disease that causes her debilitating pain in the neck and upper body. The pain kept her from doing many of the things she loved to do, and I watched as she fought to make adjustments to her new reality. This became the whole family's struggle as well—particularly my dad's. He felt responsible not only to provide for his family but to research and pursue medical care for my mother, make sure we kids had what we needed, and adapt to a life with serious limitations. My mom's illness changed her life—and all our lives—in a quantum way.

Gradually, Mom accepted her illness and the pain it caused, along with the call she felt God had given her in this new season: to pray for those God brought to her mind. This is a call she has faithfully pursued for the past forty-five years, and I'm grateful my mother's prayers have blanketed our family—and many other families—for four generations. I want my legacy to be like my parents'—with Christ as its foundation, living in a way that demonstrates a love for Jesus.

A PATH FORWARD

When I graduated from high school, I headed to college in Oklahoma. My grandpa had very specific ideas about how I should present myself at college, so he took me shopping and purchased my college wardrobe. Once again, his taste was impeccable. I can't imagine what I might have looked like as an incoming freshman, left to my own fashion devices, but Grandpa Bradbury made sure I projected a look that was classic, elegant, and a little modern. I might have been nervous about how hard college might be, but my wardrobe gave me a little boost of confidence.

Over the next four years, I pursued my bachelor's in business. For my senior year capstone project, my team was tasked with helping a local business find ways to improve their sales and processes—a lofty goal for twenty-one-year-olds with no business experience. But with all the overconfidence of youth, I set out to help.

We were assigned a local store that sold and rented musical instruments, and I was tasked to give input in the area of marketing. When I stepped into the store to meet the owner, I saw violins, guitars, pianos, flutes, and clarinets cluttered everywhere, in poorly lit displays. They were dusty, disorganized, and overcrowded.

I interviewed the owner to learn about her business and to find out what kind of improvements she wanted to see.

"Sales are lagging," she said.

After listening to her struggles and vision, I offered a suggestion. "Musical instruments are such things of

A college graduate—and yet my real education was about to begin.

beauty," I said. "If we organized them by type and then displayed them artfully, I think we could help customers respond emotionally. They would want one of your beautiful instruments in their lives."

The owner gave me free rein to reorganize the place. I did my best to create an artistic experience for customers—one that would inspire them toward making music with the instruments in her store.

I also encouraged the owner to make her storefront more inviting for passersby. This was before the days of CAD (computer-aided design) programs, so in a throwback to my sixth-grade art project, I pulled out my graph paper, ruler, pencil, and eraser and drew sketches of some simple changes she could make to the layout of the store.

The work came easily, and when I was finished, the sketches surprised me with their artistic beauty. My senior project passed muster with our department head, and I was one step closer to graduating.

Something beyond classwork had been occupying much of my time during my senior year. I had met the man who would become my husband—the same man who, a few years into our future, would decide to quit his job—a turning point that would launch my career in interior design.

GOOD DESIGN: *Choose Fine Things*

Grandpa Bradbury taught me the value of choosing classic style and quality over cheaply constructed, trendy fashion. Looking back, I can see how deeply his values affected my thinking in design—and in life. Quality has staying power.

I choose the highest quality materials or house I can afford, even if it means buying something used and in need of restoration. I invest in things that are well constructed, made with quality materials.

Quality matters in relationships, as well. When we choose fine people to walk alongside us in life, we choose well. I didn't know where the future would take me, but I knew I wanted Dale at my side. He was made of quality stuff, and somehow we would find a path forward that allowed both of us to thrive.

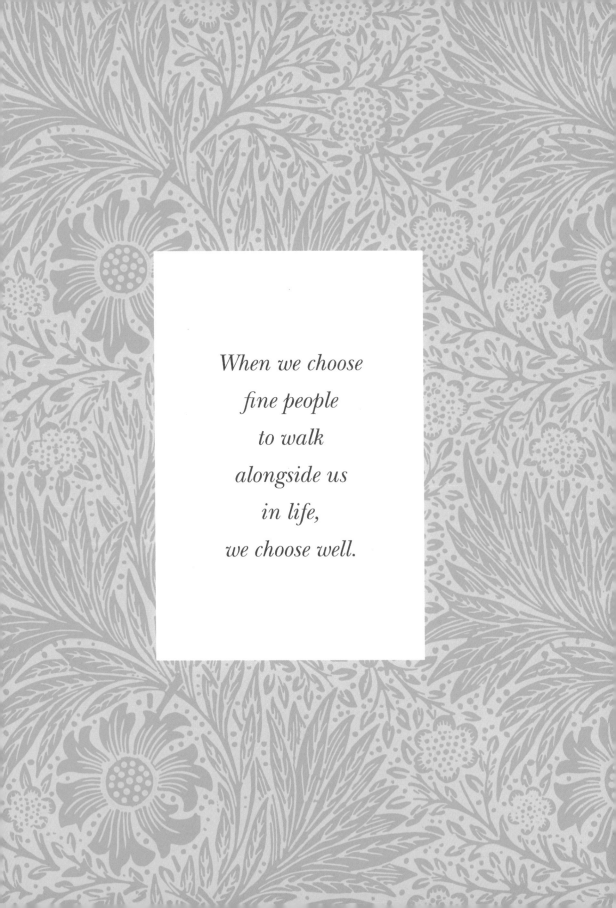

When we choose
fine people
to walk
alongside us
in life,
we choose well.

Chapter 2

BEGINNINGS

I first met Dale on a group date in college. *This guy is cute!* I thought. He was tall, athletic, and fun.

We began the evening by attending a Friday-night worship service at the university's chapel—not exactly a hot spot for the dating scene, but a nice way to begin the weekend. Afterward we went to dinner at IHOP, just a few blocks north of campus—and within range of our college-student budgets.

Dale was easy to talk to. He was a few years older than I was, earning his master's degree in business. He didn't dominate the conversation but often had funny or interesting things to add. By the end of dinner, he had my full attention. We paid our bills and headed for the door.

Once we stepped outside, the evening breeze must have caught Dale's attention, because he looked down at his pants, then looked up at me in a panic.

"My fly's open!" he said, reaching for the zipper. "I wonder if it's been open all night!"

"Only halfway," I said. *Oh my gosh. Did I really just say that? Now he knows I looked at his fly!*

"Well, thanks for cluing me in!" he said, laughing and zipping up his pants.

My cheeks burned, but Dale just smiled and took it all in stride, continuing the conversation. Maybe that's what was so appealing about him: he didn't take himself too seriously.

From that first night, Dale struck me as easygoing and the sort of person who gets genuine joy from doing helpful things for those around him. I like being helpful, too, but personality-wise we couldn't be more different.

Dale is laid back. He likes to wait and see, whereas I like to jump in with both feet. I like to feel productive—to a fault—whereas Dale likes to engage in hobbies that stimulate his mind, like chess. Who has time for chess? I like to play by the rules, but Dale doesn't always feel the need—as I soon discovered when he picked me up for a date.

"Do you know how to drive a stick?" Dale asked. He was driving his Toyota Celica, which had a manual transmission.

"Yes! My dad thought all of us kids needed to know how—'an important life skill,' he said." I was kind of proud of myself.

"Great! But can you shift gears without using the clutch?"

"What? No! You're supposed to depress the clutch and then—"

"Watch this!"

And with that, Dale moved the stick from third gear into fourth . . . without using the clutch.

"What are you doing! You can't do that!" I protested. But the car's engine slipped seamlessly into the higher gear.

"You just have to listen for when the engine is ready to change gears," he said, smirking.

I was horrified by his unconventional driving methods. And Dale was completely delighted at my shocked response to his stunt.

This was classic Dale-and-Jean dynamics. His easygoing, playful nature mellows my stronger, rule-following personality, and my inner drive provides the extra push he sometimes appreciates.

We clicked immediately and spent almost every day together the rest of that year. We were married the following October.

During our engagement, Dale followed in his father's footsteps by becoming a commodities broker and trader. Trading commodities is a complicated business that requires financial backing to get started, which his dad provided. Dale traded on the floor of the Chicago Mercantile Exchange in an "open outcry" format.

The floor was open from 7 a.m. to 2 p.m., Monday through Friday, and those seven hours were high risk and beyond hectic. Dale put his own money on the line every day, with the ever-looming prospect of losing everything with one bad trade decision. When the market closed, there was no more work to be done that day, so Dale's hours weren't long, but they were stressful.

"We alone have an imprint of what constitutes God. And since God created humans, we should assume that part of the human mission is, in turn, to create."

MARIE MUTSUKI MOCKETT

It turned out Dale was good at trading commodities, and the money he made was very good, which gave me some breathing room to figure out the next move for my own career.

After graduating from college, I'd spent weeks looking for a job—any job—in business, but I couldn't find anything. Instead, I was waitressing. It was 1982, and the economy was in a recession. The unemployment rate was 10.8 percent—the highest since the Great Depression. No one was hiring.

One afternoon that summer, I talked to my dad about my job dilemma. "No one is hiring," I lamented. "I can't even get an interview."

"I've been thinking about your situation," he said. "Have you ever considered becoming a real estate agent? Even during a recession, people are still relocating. They need to sell their houses and buy new ones, so agents are still busy. I think you'd be really good at it."

Hmm. Real estate certainly sounded more professional than waitressing. "Definitely worth looking into, Dad," I said. "Thanks!"

The more I thought about Dad's idea, the more I liked it. The next day I signed up for a course to get my Illinois real estate license. I passed the exam, and

*Newlyweds ready to take on
the world—with a 1980s
bowl cut and mustache!*

one of my instructors offered me a desk to begin my new career. By the time Dale and I were married that October, I was showing homes to two new customers.

Showing houses was fun, and it exposed me to many different styles of homes. Occasionally I showed a home that really stood out. The homeowners clearly had style. Their furniture selections, color palettes, lighting fixtures, and décor had been carefully thought through, which gave the home a cohesive, dramatic vibe.

HOMEOWNERS

The lease on our apartment would be up soon, and Dale and I hoped to buy a home as soon as we could afford it. Mortgage rates had dropped recently—a mere 12.5 percent (compared to 21 percent just two years before!). I found a town house in Oak Park, a suburb west of Chicago. It was close enough to the Chicago Mercantile Exchange that Dale could easily take the train to work. This unit was new construction—the model home of a new development of town houses. It had two bedrooms and a luxurious two and a half baths.

I wrote up a sales contract and made an offer, which the builder accepted. We secured a mortgage, and just like that, we were homeowners.

My head was filled with ideas from the stylish homes I'd seen at work, and this town house was ripe for design. It was, in a word, beige. Beige walls, beige carpeting, and honey-oak cabinets and trim. The place had zero personality, but it was ours, and I was so excited to have a place of our own.

I enjoyed my real estate job, but my work was mostly during the evenings and weekends—the opposite of Dale's hours. The markets were open from 7 a.m. to 2 p.m., period. After I had been in real estate for a year, Dale and I began to wonder whether it would be better for us as a couple if our hours were more compatible.

I started looking for a part-time job with daytime hours. Since Dale's income was enough to support us, I had flexibility about the kinds of jobs I could consider. When I was offered an office manager position at an interior design firm, I said yes.

Working for the design firm threw me into a job I had little experience in—but plenty of interest in. The owners were two women fresh out of design school, and I was excited to be their first employee. It paid a whopping $3.85 an hour, but the hours were perfect: 9 a.m. to 1 p.m., Monday through Friday. I'd be home when Dale was home.

I love a good challenge, and this job didn't disappoint. Dressed in classic business clothes I'd purchased under the advisement of Grandpa Bradbury (and sporting a brand-new perm), I looked very professional at twenty-three years of age. In the coming months, I gained skills in writing contracts, placing orders, paying bills, invoicing, and dealing with workrooms (the workshops where designer upholstery, draperies, and home furnishings are created).

I'd known next to nothing about interior design when I started that job, and it opened my eyes to a whole new world. I now realized that those houses I'd shown people as a real estate agent—the ones that really popped—had likely been professionally designed by an interior designer. The paint, flooring, window treatments, and furniture all worked beautifully together. Even the home decor, from art to throw pillows, fit into the same cohesive look and feel. And the materials used—the upholstery fabrics, rugs, and furnishings—all were "fine things." I was discovering that interior design was a practical, functional form of art.

All that beige in our town house was a blank canvas screaming for design. Neither Dale nor I knew anything about remodeling. Our families had never remodeled their homes, and they hired professionals whenever repairs were needed. But what we lacked in skill, we made up for in sheer determination.

We pulled up the beige carpet and hired someone to install hardwood floors. I wanted our plain walls to look paneled, so I bought a hand miter saw, cut strips of molding to size, and attached them to the wall with a hot-glue gun. It worked!

We removed a decorative railing that separated our living and dining rooms, and I loved how it opened the space. We even installed green marble on the fireplace (don't judge me—it was the eighties!).

I worked my way through the home, painting every room. I sewed curtains from floral fabric I'd bought in a color scheme that was cutting edge for the era—celadon green and peach, which perfectly matched my closet full of cowl-neck sweaters and work blazers with amply padded shoulders.

When the curtains were hung, I called for Dale. "Come see!"

"Wow, Jean, they look great!" he said. "I can't believe what a difference this makes."

"Thanks!" I said, grinning. "So, how would you feel about helping me hang wallpaper?"

We spent the next Saturday wallpapering the bathroom—a five-foot-by-five-foot space, which isn't much elbow room for two adults who had never remodeled anything before. We generously slathered wallpaper paste onto the back of the strips and hung them carefully in place, trimming away the excess paper with an X-Acto knife. There were a few tense moments, but we survived.

After the last strip was hung, we stood back and surveyed our handiwork, feeling very proud of ourselves.

"We are awesome," Dale said.

I totally agreed.

The next morning when I stepped into the bathroom, I discovered all the wallpaper had slid off the walls and onto the floor. It turns out you're supposed to treat the walls with something called sizing before applying the wallpaper. Who knew?

I was really pleased with how the town house turned out, and the remodeling process had been relatively smooth (minus the wallpaper situation). What surprised me was how much fun I'd had transforming our bland, beige town house into a modern, beautiful (for the 1980s) home.

THE BVILDING

At church one day, a friend approached Dale and me with an idea. He was a general contractor, and he'd been eyeing a rundown building that he thought had potential.

"Want to go fifty-fifty with me in buying an old boardinghouse?" he asked. "The building is currently condemned—"

"Condemned?" I interjected.

"Don't worry—it has good bones. It's located in the historic district, and if we can prove that the house has enough architectural value to be considered 'contributing to the historic district,' then every dollar we spend on its remodel would earn us a tax credit."

"Tax credit?" Dale asked. Now he was talking Dale's language.

"I think it's big enough to create four rental apartments," our friend continued. "It's in a great location, with a strong rental market. Plus, it's close to the train station, so people who work downtown would have an easy commute. I don't think we'd have any problem keeping it rented."

"So, how are you envisioning this partnership working?" I asked.

"I'm thinking you would provide half the financial backing, and I'd provide the other half. Our newly formed partnership would hire my construction company to do the work. If you want to, you could help with how the place looks."

Interesting.

"You've made me curious," Dale said.

I could see nothing but green lights. Dale needed time to process this from a financial point of view. He's always provided a good set of brakes to my foot-on-the-gas reflex.

We spent a few days talking it over with our parents and a few trusted friends who knew the real estate market. By the end of the week, we decided we were in. Our friend made a joint offer of $84,000 on the old building, which was accepted. Just like that, we were the proud co-owners of a condemned boardinghouse.

The building was on South Boulevard in Oak Park, not far from our town house. Many of the old stone buildings in nearby downtown Chicago had the name of the building carved above their stone entrances. In the popular font of that era, the letter *u* was often written as a *v*, so Dale and I began referring to the boardinghouse as "the Bvilding" (pronounced *buh-VIL-ding*).

The Bvilding, a large two-story, clapboard Italianate Victorian, had a certain amount of curb appeal if you squinted your eyes just right, but when we stepped inside . . . man, did it reek. It smelled like stale cigarettes, rotting food, and bathrooms that hadn't been cleaned in a very long time.

A maze of hallways connected tiny bedrooms, with a single bath on each floor and a kitchen downstairs. It would take a lot of wall-moving to turn that rabbit warren of rooms into four apartments. The crew began their work.

The Bvilding—my first opportunity to draft a real floor plan and choose paint colors.

Our new business partner reached out to me. "It's time to plan the layout for the four kitchens and baths. Want to give it a stab?" he asked.

"Glad to!" I replied. I knew nothing about how to draft a real floor plan, but I was good with a ruler, a pencil, and—especially—an eraser.

"Could you choose the cabinets and carpeting too? And the paint colors? Inside and out?"

"Sure!" I had no reason whatsoever to feel confident. I had no training and little experience. But I love a new challenge, and I was sure I could figure it out.

At the design firm, I was an absolute sponge. I loved listening to my bosses, Donna and Joyce, brainstorm with clients about their upcoming projects. It was as if they spoke another language, filled with words and phrases I'd never heard, like *railroaded fabric* and *drapery fullness*. I admired how their company helped transform people's houses into beautiful homes.

DRAWING LESSONS

Donna noticed my growing passion for design, and one morning she stopped by my desk.

"Jean, if you're at all interested in design, you probably need to learn how to draft," she said, "I think you should sign up for a drafting class."

That afternoon I drove over to our local junior college to find out what was available. I enrolled in a drafting class that started in the fall.

I loved every minute of it. My book list for the class included a textbook and the basic tools of drafting, which I bought at an art supply store: drafting pencils and a sharpener, stencils, a T square, drafting paper, and a portable drafting board. But perhaps the most important tool I bought that day was a brand-new eraser.

I learned to twirl the pencil as I drew so the line would be the same thickness for the entire length. I learned the correct way to form capital letters to label my designs. I learned how to draw and diagram windows, doors, fireplaces, and walls. When the class progressed to drawing foundation walls and roof structures, I dropped out. I'd learned what I needed to know—how to draw proper floor plans. I was ready to put my new skills into practice.

When it was time to design the kitchens and baths in the Bvilding, I was more ready than I'd been a couple of months ago. I measured each room, dreamed up how I wanted each kitchen to look, then got out my tools and began drawing.

I presented the finished plans—four unique custom kitchens and four unique baths—to our friend and business partner.

"These will work," he said. Knowing his understated personality, I hadn't expected a big pat on the back, but when he added, "I'll send your layouts to my cabinet guy," I felt like a real professional. I turned my focus to picking out carpeting, vinyl flooring, and paint colors for both inside and out.

By the time we placed a "For Rent" ad in the local paper, the Bvilding gleamed. The four units rented out quickly, and I felt the satisfaction of seeing the project through to completion. I loved how we'd retained the original look and feel of the Bvilding while making it safe, usable, and attractive for a new generation.

Best of all, it no longer reeked.

The Historic Preservation Department of Oak Park certified the Bvilding as "contributing to the historic district," which meant we got tax credit for the money we'd spent. I was happy, and so was Dale—with everything except his job, as I would soon find out.

⬡ GOOD BUSINESS: *Questions to Ask before Buying Rental Property*

Dale and I learned a ton about real estate investment when we copurchased the Bvilding. It was my first attempt at drawing up floor plans for a remodel and only the second time I'd designed the aesthetic of a home (the first being our town house).

People often ask me how to tell if a run-down house is a good real estate investment. Entire books, television shows, and professional courses are dedicated to this topic, and I would never try to offer a comprehensive list. But here are some key questions Dale and I have learned to ask before making an offer on an investment property.

- *Does the house have good bones?* Is it structurally sound? Many challenges can be overcome in a neglected house as long as it has a solid foundation and framework. Be sure to have the house inspected by a professional who knows how to check for things like active foundation cracks and sagging beams.

- *Can you recoup the cost of remodeling?* How much do comparable units rent for in your area? Can you fund needed repairs and remodeling costs up front—and pay down the mortgage with the help of the rent payments over time? If the house sits empty for a few months, do you have the financial stability to absorb the lost income?

- *Is the house in a hot rental market?* Does it stand out? Is it near a university where students need housing? Is it near public transportation? Is it in a safe neighborhood? Extra points for a fenced yard.

- *How much of the repair and remodeling can you do yourself?* If the work is cosmetic, you can save money by doing those upgrades yourself and only hiring out for repairs that require permits and a trained professional. YouTube and Pinterest offer a huge variety of tutorials on how to complete DIY projects.

- *How many stories are there?* It's very difficult and expensive to get workers who are willing to paint the third story of a house or replace the roof of a tall house. We prefer houses that are one or two stories.

- *How easily can you manage the property once it's rented?* Is it close to where you live or work so you can easily keep an eye on it? Is the house complicated by a lot of systems that can go wrong? The simpler the house, the less headache it will be to manage.

Providing homes for families through well-tended rental properties is satisfying work—and can bring valuable income so long as you choose your property wisely.

Chapter 3

OF BUSINESS & BABIES

As soon as Dale and I got home from that fateful Florida vacation when he told me he was leaving his job, he began the process of extricating himself from the high-stress world of commodities trading. He sold his seat on the Exchange, put the money in the bank, and began his "chapter 2," trying to figure out what he wanted to do next.

I went back to work, knowing I needed to figure out how to earn more money. My part-time, minimum-wage job wouldn't sustain us for long.

I'd learned so much from Donna and Joyce during my time in their office. I'd experimented with actual design on two projects: the kitchens and baths of our Bvilding and the complete redecoration of our town house. I was proud of how those projects had turned out. My friends told me our home was beautiful and began asking for my design advice on their houses.

One busy morning at work, a woman named Carolyn called. I recognized her voice immediately. She was a friend of my mom's and had been my vacation Bible school teacher when I was a kid.

"Hey, Jean," she said. "Here's the deal: now that our youngest is off to college, all five of our kids are out of the house. My poor home is exhausted, and it needs a good redecorating."

"Let me make an appointment for you with Donna and Joyce," I said. "You'll love them."

"No—wait. Jean, I don't want to talk with one of your designers," she said. "I want you! When I visited you and Dale at Christmas, I couldn't help but notice how beautiful your town house is, and I hear you designed it yourself. True?"

"Well, yes."

"That's what I want you to do for me! Let's work together. I love your taste. You have a good eye."

"Thanks!" I said. "I'll be happy to take a look." *How fun it would be to design her home! And I'm pretty sure I could earn more than minimum wage on this project.*

Carolyn and I set up a time to meet at her house, and she showed me everything she was hoping to redecorate.

I could see right away what she meant by "exhausted." Her house had been a hub house—the place where kids and families had gathered over the years. That wonderful activity created a lot of wear and tear. The carpeting was faded, the walls showcased years' worth of handprints, and the upholstery on her furniture was wearing thin. But her home had tons of potential.

As I took notes in each room, ideas began popping into my mind.

"I think I can help you," I told her. "We'll need to reupholster some furniture, select paint colors and wallpaper, and choose carpeting. I'll send you a design contract that covers the scope of services." I was grateful to be able to apply the knowledge I'd gained from working at the design firm.

When I got home, I told Dale how exciting the meeting with Carolyn had been. "I can't wait to get started," I said. "I think I'll set up a little office in the spare bedroom."

"Great!" Dale said. "I'll help."

"I wonder what Donna and Joyce will think," I mused. "They got their degrees in interior design before they started designing. Here I am, jumping in headfirst with only half of a drafting class and a couple of personal projects under my belt."

Dale looked me straight in the eye. "Jean, you can totally do this job," he said. "You might not have formal training, but you have a gift. You have a good eye for design, and you can figure things out like no one I've ever met. Just look what you did here!" He motioned around the room. Our little town house was seriously cute. "And look what you did to the Bvilding!" he continued, gaining momentum. "That building was in way worse shape than Carolyn's house. You've got this."

I sent Carolyn the contract, and a few days later I received an envelope in the mail. My first signed contract—and a deposit for design services. *This makes it official!*

At work, Donna knew I'd taken on a freelance job. She gave me her blessing because I'd been approached by a family friend and not through my role at the firm.

I couldn't believe how much fun I was having each evening, dreaming up ideas for Carolyn's house. She loved the samples of paint, fabrics, and carpeting I brought by. We made a few tweaks, and she signed off on all the selections.

> *"God does not require that we be successful, only that we be faithful."*
>
> MOTHER TERESA

In order to get trade-only pricing on materials needed for the job, I needed to set myself up as a business.

"I need to give the business a name," I told Dale one evening as I filled out paperwork for my new sole proprietorship. "I'm thinking 'Jean Stoffer Interiors.'"

"Incredibly creative," he said with a smile. "Go for it!"

And so Jean Stoffer Interiors was born.

I finished Carolyn's house in just a few weeks. The new flooring, fresh color palette, and flood of natural light that came pouring through the windows gave the whole home a happy, fresh feel.

When the last bit of work was done, Carolyn and I stood in her living room and looked around.

"I love it!" she said. "This was money well spent." We hugged, and she paid me for the completed project.

Carolyn's home would continue being a hub home. With her kids off to college and starting families of their own, her living room would be party central for bridal showers, baby showers, and anniversary parties. It felt good to envision the memories yet to be made in her living room and kitchen—and to know I'd played a small part.

On my way home, I stopped by the bank to deposit the check. My fun little side job had just added nicely to our bank balance. I thought back to our Florida vacation and my prayer during the flight home. Was this God's way of showing me what he wanted me to do next?

DALE'S SALES

As Dale began searching for a new career path, my dad approached him about an opportunity. Dad was launching a business that sold inventory management systems, and he was looking for a likable, trustworthy salesman to help him get started. He offered Dale the position.

"You'll get a percentage of the profit for every system you sell," Dad told him. "I'd love to have you on board, even if it's just temporary. I think you'd be good at sales."

"It's a new kind of role for me," he said, "but let's give it a try and see how it goes. Thank you, Dad!"

It went well. Dale's honest, friendly personality made him a natural at sales.

The systems Dale was selling were five-figure contracts, and when he made his first sale, my dad gave him 100 percent of the profit—$7,500, which was significant in 1980. It was a big deal to us.

"To help you kids get started," he explained.

We were so grateful. Dad's willingness to bring Dale on board helped my husband discover he really loved sales—and he was good at it.

After six months of working with my dad, Dale ended up taking a job in industrial sales, selling commercial packaging materials. It was a great fit with good people, and he got to work from home, which was a rarity in the 1980s. Granted, his salary was a 90 percent pay cut from what he'd been earning on the floor in commodities. But Dale's new job was doable for our family, and more important, he liked it.

WORD OF MOUTH

Word of mouth is the best possible advertising for a new business, and Carolyn was to be a fantastic promoter. She frequently invited friends over, and she loved giving them a tour of her newly redecorated home.

"Jean Stoffer helped me with all of this," she would say. "Would you like her number?"

Soon my phone was ringing, and new clients were signing up for redecorating. "Thanks for introducing me to the 'Empty Nest Express,'" I told her.

I loved working with clients and capturing the look they wanted for their homes. I was always struck by what a difference paint, carpeting, upholstery, and window treatments could make when they were thoughtfully appointed.

With the additional design jobs, the rental income from the Bvilding, and Dale's salary from his new job, I decided to quit the design firm and go full time with Jean Stoffer Interiors. I put in my two weeks' notice and thanked my bosses for everything they'd taught me.

That evening over dinner, I looked at Dale and said, "Here we go." I had found a new line of work: redecorating homes.

GROWING NUMBERS

Dale and I had always wanted a family and were thrilled when we learned we were expecting. We'd been married for three years, and the timing seemed perfect.

My urge to nest came on strong, but our spare bedroom was currently my office—and Dale's, since he worked from home most days. Where would our baby go?

"I think we should move," I said to Dale one morning.

"Again?" he protested. "We've only lived here for two years."

"I know, but we'll need a room for the baby, and wouldn't it be nice to own a little house with a yard?"

"I'm quite comfortable here," Dale said.

"I'll just take a look at what's on the market."

We found a little house on Monroe Avenue in nearby River Forest that had good bones but was, once again, beige. Its main selling points? Three bedrooms, a fenced backyard, and a fresh canvas just waiting for a decorator's touch. We sold our town house, bought the Monroe house, and in April of that year, we moved in.

On our budget, we couldn't dive into remodeling the whole house at once. Instead, we tackled one room at a time. With a baby due in a couple of months, the nursery took priority. We wallpapered the room (hiring a professional this time!) and took up the living room carpet carefully so we could reuse it in baby's room. To our delight, we discovered hardwood floors underneath!

Carolyn hosted a baby shower for me in her living room—the first room I'd professionally redecorated. I was happy and proud on so many levels the day of that shower.

Our baby boy was born in July, and we named him David. If ever there is something that will remodel your life, it's the birth of a child. From day one, David was a live wire. He felt sleep was overrated and was only content when we kept him moving. My new baby stroller and I developed a serious relationship.

I loved our little guy with my whole heart, and I was happy to have traded my business clothes for jeans and a T-shirt—and to have a work-from-home job that made it possible for me to be with David.

START SMALL

Adjusting to sleepless nights, nursing, and the omnipresent demands of a tiny human is no small feat for any parent. It wasn't until the following spring that I was ready to tackle a little remodeling project in our new home.

Dale traveled regularly for his new job, and during one such trip, I thought I'd surprise him by beginning renovation on the only full bathroom in our house. *It's a small room. How hard can it be?*

I thought I'd switch out the wall tile and began removing the tiles. One thing led to another, and by the time I was done, I had successfully rendered our bathroom unusable.

Let's just say Dale was surprised when he got home. With the drywall now exposed around the tub, we couldn't use the shower. Luckily, we lived near an

The Monroe house, where our kids had a yard to play in and I got to dabble with design.

Enjoying the fruits of my labor at my baby shower in Carolyn's newly designed living room.

Leaving the hospital with baby David to begin my new (and favorite) job: motherhood.

athletic club we'd joined. For the entire summer, we walked the three blocks to use their showers—an oh-so-simple solution with a stroller and a ten-month-old baby in tow.

I learned the hard way that the timing of a remodel project is like choreography. Certain things need to happen in a certain order—and ripping out the house's only shower isn't the ideal place to start! Note to self: before beginning demolition, carefully consider how it will affect the family living in the home.

Eventually the bathroom got put back together, tile and all.

"It's sure nice to take a shower without having to load up a stroller," Dale quipped.

Point taken. But boy, did I love our bathroom's new look! *Worth it!*

The price of real estate had picked up nicely since we bought and remodeled the Bvilding. We decided to sell our half of the investment, and with that money, we almost paid off the mortgage on our little house.

Dale was elated. "We're almost debt free," he said. "What a great feeling!"

When Dale wasn't traveling, he worked from home. It was the perfect pairing with my interiors business, which continued to keep me busy. If Dale was home, I could slip away when David was napping. If Dale was out of town, I would use the evenings to replenish myself by sewing, doing cross-stitch, or reading.

No drywall? No problem. Finally—a working tub!

My job description expands with baby number two, John.

When David was twenty-one months old, we added another baby to the family: sweet John. Three years after that, I was pregnant again.

"We've maxed out the space in this house," I said to Dale. "Three kids and two work-from-home offices will be a little tight."

Dale looked at me, alarm in his eyes. "No—we're not moving again," he said, reading my mind. "Our mortgage here is almost paid off! In another year or two, we can live here practically for free." Imagining such a happy day, he gazed out the window and sighed.

"Why don't I just look and see what's on the market?" I suggested.

Over the years I had learned that Dale and I could never come to a decision on something while it was just a concept. For the next several months, I checked out houses on the market, hoping Dale would agree to move if I found the right one.

Before beginning demolition, carefully consider how it will affect the family living in the home.

"If we move, let's buy a house that will last us," he said. "This is our final house, promise?"

"Promise." And with that, I became a woman on a mission.

GOOD BUSINESS: *Grow Your Business by Word of Mouth*

Nothing attracts new clients like solid word-of-mouth referrals. What can you do to grow your business by word of mouth?

- *Go above and beyond.* Do the kind of quality work that leaves your clients pleasantly surprised. Do a little more than promised and do it with the utmost integrity.

- *Be grateful.* Send a Christmas present or housewarming gift to your client. Tell them you're thankful they chose to work with you.

- *Share photos.* Clients love to see beautiful images of their home. If you've taken photos of their project—whether professional shots or the ones you took with your phone—share the gallery with them.

- *Respond.* If a past client has a problem down the road with something you helped them with, do what you can to help them solve the problem.

- *Be easy to find.* Keep your website up to date and easy to navigate so clients can easily connect with you. Use social media to showcase your work, keeping it fresh and professional.

⬡ GOOD BUSINESS: *Write a Solid Contract*

Even though my first design job was with Carolyn, a longtime friend, I still wrote up a contract so we were clear on what was expected. Getting things in writing prevents awkward conversations and misunderstandings later on. (If you're unsure about writing a contract or your project is complex, consult a lawyer who specializes in business law.)

Here are items I include in every design contract:

- *Scope of work:* Which rooms will I be working in? What selections will I be making for those rooms, and what won't be included? Examples include space planning, cabinetry layouts and design, appliance selection, lighting and plumbing selection and placement, tile selection, countertop and hardware selection, millwork designs, furnishings, and wall, window, and floor coverings.

- *Purchase of finish materials:* I list the categories of finish materials we provide for our projects, such as cabinetry, lighting fixtures, and furnishings. I describe the ordering process, the deposits required, and whether things are nonrefundable.

- *Design fee:* I charge a flat design fee based on square footage of the space(s) to be designed.

- *Payment:* I ask for 50 percent of the design fee and a signed contract up front. The next 25 percent is due upon final selection of materials, and the last 25 percent is due upon project completion. (This doesn't include finish material purchases such as cabinetry or furnishings. I handle those with separate price quotes, followed by invoices once the quote is accepted.) For items that are in stock, I require 100 percent payment up front to place the order. For custom orders, I require a 75 percent deposit, with the final 25 percent required to release items for delivery. I've learned the hard way how costly it can be to deliver custom-ordered items only to have a client not pay for them.

Taking the time to write a clear, professional contract saves time and countless headaches. Writing down exactly what's being promised by me and expected from the client keeps misunderstandings to a minimum and allows everyone to enjoy the design process.

◩ GOOD LIVING: *Work from Home with Kids*

My career as a designer and business owner began during the throes of having babies and raising kids. If you are a parent who works from home, how do you uphold both priorities—caring for your children and keeping your word to clients?

As I practiced the juggling act of prioritizing my family while growing a business, I relied on four opportunities to get my work done:

- *Naptimes:* When babies slept, I shifted gears and pulled out my design work. Sometimes other chores demanded my attention or a baby refused to nap (yes, David, I'm talking about you), but for the most part, I could depend on naptimes to get at least a little design work done during the day when our kids were young.

- *Bedtimes:* Dale and I put our kids to bed early. Kids—especially young children and teens—need a lot of sleep. You know who else benefited from our kids' early bedtimes? Me! I counted on those evenings to get uninterrupted chunks of design work done or just to be an off-duty grownup.

- *School:* Once my kids started school, I thought I'd have way more time on my hands. Instead, I discovered I was just a different kind of busy. I hadn't accounted for two things: (1) school involves lots of activities, sporting events, and smiling through fourth-grade recorder concerts; and (2) parenting older kids takes relational time and energy, especially during the teen years. Nonetheless, once my mom-of-preschoolers days were behind me, it was easier to get design work done during school days so I could be fully present with the kids when they got home. Being my kids' mom was the most fulfilling investment I've ever made, and I wouldn't trade any of it.

- *Outside help:* With little kids at home and a small business to run, I was constantly buried under a mountain of housework. My sister, a former missionary in Southeast Asia, finally sat me down. "You can't do it all, Jeannie. Hire outside help. It's a worthy investment." I found a gifted housekeeper, and it was a game changer. Eva would do laundry, pick up toys, make beds, do dishes, vacuum, and sweep. I was then free to put my best energies into my kids and my business. If you can make this work in your budget, go for it. You'll never look back.

Chapter 4

THE UGLIEST HOUSE
IN TOWN

My house-hunting mission got a major boost when I received a call from a friend who was the village assessor in River Forest. She knew the inside scoop on everything related to local real estate.

"I might have an off-market house for you to look at," she said.

I was all ears.

One phone call later, Dale and I had an appointment to see the house. It was located exactly where we wanted to live—smack-dab in the middle of River Forest. It had four bedrooms, one bath, and a huge attic—but because of its condition, it was affordable.

We made our way up the front walk, and the closer we got, the worse the house looked. Some sort of awful greenish asphalt–like roofing shingles—was nailed to the house as siding. Cheap, dull aluminum storm windows covered the original glass, and evergreen bushes obscured the entire front of the house.

The Victorian house had been built in 1891, so I had expected to see charming, sweeping porches at the front and side entrances. At some point in the past hundred years, however, the porches had been replaced with concrete stoops and rusty rails.

We knocked on the heavy front door, and the owners invited us in.

My heart leaped when I stepped inside and saw a spectacular staircase and ten-foot ceilings. We toured the house and discovered it was in solid shape—no water damage, no insect damage—and the basic floor plan was appealing. On the downside, the house had an oil-burning boiler and no air-conditioning, the original cabinetry wasn't in great shape, and the plumbing fixtures and appliances were on their last legs.

Once we were back outside, Dale gave his assessment: "It's like a gift wrapped in a garbage bag."

Pretty accurate assessment, I thought. "But it's solid and it has more than enough room for our growing family. I'm already getting excited about the design opportunities. We can work with this."

"Fine," Dale said. "But seriously, I do not want to move again after this. Let's stay put and raise our family here. It's a nice neighborhood, and this house will keep us busy with projects for years to come. Deal?"

"Deal."

We called the owners and made a contingent offer. The owners accepted, so we listed and sold our little house. Sixty days later, we were the happy owners of a run-down Victorian on Lathrop Avenue in River Forest.

It was ninety-four degrees on our moving day. The house had no air-conditioning, and I was six months pregnant. Somehow those four flights of stairs, from basement to attic, seemed less spectacular than when we'd toured the house.

When the last moving boxes were finally unloaded into our new home, Dale presented me with a piece of paper.

"What's this?" I asked.

"Read it," he said with a smirk.

"'I, Jean Stoffer, do solemnly swear that I will never ask to move again,'" I read.

He pulled a pen from his shirt pocket and handed it to me. "Sign."

"Serious?"

"Serious. Sign."

I signed. He then drove to the bank and placed the contract in our safe-deposit box, where it sat untouched for the next twenty-five years.

We were home.

LATHROP

I loved being a work-from-home mom, and I found satisfaction in my career. I only took on a few projects at a time, but they earned enough to fund the projects in our Lathrop house and then some. During naptimes and after the kids went to bed, I'd sketch designs or tackle Lathrop projects.

If I needed to visit a client's jobsite when Dale was unavailable to watch the children, I packed along a baby or toddler or hired a sitter.

I felt fortunate to pursue work that inspired me, but the greatest gift I could give my children was to invest my best hours in being their mom.

The Lathrop house, with its ghastly green asphalt-shingle siding. A diamond in the rough.

I volunteered in my kids' classrooms and taught their Sunday school classes. I was a room mom for each child one time. I also carted them to endless sports activities and cheered for them while Dale coached.

What kept me sane during those oh-so-busy years of raising little kids was the women I got to know through the moms' groups at my church—especially my dear friend Jill, whose kids were the same ages as my own. We would often call each other for a check-in during "arsenic hour"—that window of time right before dinner, when everyone is crabby. Babies would be crying on both ends of the line. Here's how our conversations would go:

"Hi. What are you making tonight?"

"Spaghetti. You?"

"Macaroni and cheese."

"Perfect. Have a great night!"

"You, too!"

"Bye!"

"Bye!"

We were two young moms in the same foxhole, reaching across the phone line to remind each other we weren't alone. Those calls meant the world to me. In fact, one of the big attractions about our new home on Lathrop was that it was right down the street from Jill's house.

Raising children together forms a bond that lasts a lifetime, and Jill remains among my closest friends to this day.

We moved into the Lathrop house just before David started kindergarten. His school was within walking distance, and I soon became acquainted with the school's crossing guard, an older gentleman named Mr. Farber.

> *Raising children together through the years forms a bond that lasts a lifetime.*

"Are you new to the neighborhood?" he asked one day as I waited on the curb with David.

"Yes, actually," I said, introducing myself and my son. "We just bought a house over on Lathrop."

"That house with the green siding?" he asked.

"That's the one," I said.

"So you're the family who bought the ugliest house in town!" he said, laughing.

I laughed too. "You're right! That's us! But be patient. I have plans for that house."

"I used to court a girl who lived in your house back in the 1940s, when it was a beautiful place," he said. "Want me to see if she has any old photos?"

My heart skipped a beat. "Yes! Absolutely!" I couldn't wait to see what our house had looked like before its uglification days.

A few weeks later, after dropping David off at school, I spotted Mr. Farber. "I've got some pictures for you," he said, pulling a large manila envelope from beneath his coat. "Here you go. My lady friend made copies. I think you'll be pleased. She's excited to see what you'll do with her old home."

I pulled out a stack of photos and began flipping through them. "Look—the front porch!" I held up a photo taken from the front yard. "And clapboard siding instead of asphalt!"

"It didn't use to be the ugliest house in town," Mr. Farber said, smiling.

Just as I'd suspected, sprawling porches had once framed the front and side doors of the old Victorian. "These are perfect, Mr. Farber," I said. "They'll definitely help me restore the old place. Thank you so much."

The Lathrop house in 1940, with original clapboards and adorable porches.

Restoring old homes, I was learning, required a mixture of detective work and design skill. First came the sleuthing to discover what once had been. Then came the recreating of something both classic in appearance and modern in function.

BOARDINGHOUSE

As the due date of our third baby neared, I took stock of my situation. Jean Stoffer Interiors had become increasingly busy. With Dale's travel and my business, I didn't think I had it in me to be the mom my kids deserved once the baby arrived.

"I need to make a change," I said to Dale. "I want to be the kind of mom who has plenty of energy for her kids. Work will always be there, but kids grow up."

We talked and strategized about what to do. It was a long conversation but not a tense one, because we had a common goal. We both felt strongly that our kids needed more of my undivided focus.

"I don't want to shutter the business. I love it too much, and it's a career I want to continue when the kids are older. But I'm definitely retiring from this pace of life while the kids are little."

I decided to stop taking on new clients. If a former client approached me about a new project, I would say yes, which would keep my foot in the door with the business. That move alone would significantly simplify my life. But how would I replace the lost income?

Our Lathrop house had only one bathroom, but it was a roomy home. If we could rent out the two attic bedrooms to local college students, it would replace my lost business income.

I talked over the idea with Dale, and he was all in. I reached out to a local organization that arranges housing for international students, and soon our house was home to two young adults from Japan.

This arrangement worked out beautifully. The students ate dinner with us each night, and they had full "fridge rights" for making their own breakfasts and lunches. Our kids got to know students from across the world, and we got to provide a home for young adults far from their own homes.

I didn't realize how much I'd needed this slower pace. Even with the busyness of two toddlers and preparing for a third baby, my new life felt like a gift. I loved the freedom of being with the kids without the divided loyalties of having to return phone calls or prepare for presentations. This also freed up space in my head for fresh ideas, including one that would soon become my trademark in design.

Over the next four years, we welcomed a rotating stream of international students into our home—seventeen students in all, from several different countries, with all of us sharing the same bathroom.

Dale and me leaving the hospital with Grace. The kids now outnumber us!

HIDDEN BEAUTY

Grace was born on Christmas Eve, and she was an easy baby from the start. That spring I was excited to begin our remodel of the ugliest house in town.

The house was outdated, but there weren't any real emergencies that had to be fixed right away. We had a functioning kitchen and one bath—including a shower, which I knew better than to tear out until we had successfully installed a second bath.

The question was, where should we begin?

"The green siding is so gross," I said to Dale.

"I totally agree," he said. "Let's see what's underneath."

We peeked under a few green shingles, and to my delight, the original clapboards I'd seen in the photos were still there!

"Let's tear off the shingles ourselves! How hard could it be?" I asked Dale.

We borrowed my dad's thirty-foot extension ladder and stopped by the hardware store to buy tools. Then we stood next to the house, crowbars in hand, staring up at the ladder—with equal parts confidence and ignorance.

"Here we go," Dale said, stepping toward the ladder.

But I jumped in front of him and scrambled to the top. Nudging the end of my crowbar beneath a shingle, I pried it loose and watched it tumble to the ground.

"Awesome!" Dale called from below.

I brushed away decades of dust and cobwebs and examined the siding I'd exposed. "It's in decent shape!" I yelled down.

The ugly asphalt shingles had protected the original clapboards, which were a hundred years old and in need of paint but other-

Removing the asphalt siding was tricky, but we were delighted to discover the Lathrop's original clapboards underneath.

wise in good condition. Beneath its old skin, the ugliest house in town was a timeless beauty.

The shedding of shingles on a house of this size was harder than we'd imagined. After back-to-back trips to the emergency room for twin tetanus shots and bandages after each of us lost battles with rusty nails (me in the foot, Dale in his hand), we began to rethink the wisdom of our DIY approach to demolition.

"Removing this siding isn't complicated, but it takes a lot of strength," I said.

"And no fear of heights," he said. "Plus, our ratio of shingles to tetanus shots isn't great, and we've barely made a dent on this project. A crew of professionals could make quick work of this, but it will take us months. Let's hire it out."

"Works for me," I said.

We hired a construction crew, and they removed the shingles in no time flat—with zero trips to the emergency room. They made necessary repairs to the original siding and replaced the anodized aluminum storm windows with white triple-track storms.

I loved seeing the Lathrop's exterior restored to its original charm. Now, to tackle the inside!

Hiring them was one of the smartest decisions we made, saving us loads of time—and probably money, too, if we factored in the inevitable stitches and shots in our future. It was a good lesson. There was no shame in not being able to do everything ourselves. Sometimes the smartest move is to hire the right people for the job.

Because we'd gone into this project assuming (naively) we could do much of the work ourselves, the project cost much more than we'd anticipated. We didn't know to get estimates ahead of time, so we were billed for time and materials. As the project went on, it became clear that we didn't have enough money to complete the job.

Once again, my dad came to our rescue. He loaned us the money to finish what we'd started and pay our guys. Shortly thereafter, Dale got an end-of-year sales bonus—almost exactly the amount we'd borrowed—and we were able to repay my dad.

That bonus felt like God's provision. The whole experience taught us a lesson in how to budget a project accurately, and we became more careful planners for our future projects.

⬡ GOOD DESIGN: *Research a House's History*

Seeing old photos of the Lathrop house gave me a huge head start in planning our remodel. Old houses have history, and restoring a home to its original glory takes research. Think of yourself as a detective on a mission to discover your home's long-lost past.

Where do you look for your house's hidden past? Here are some resources that can steer you in the right direction.

- *Current neighbors:* Do any of the people living on your street remember your house as it used to be? Do they have photos from those days? Do they know how to contact previous owners?

- *Previous owners:* You can research the names of previous owners through your city's title office. They may or may not provide contact information, but online research may lead you to a current address or phone number. If a previous owner is willing to give you a little history, here are some questions to ask:

  - Do you have old photos of the house?

  - Was any remodeling work done to the house? Any room additions?

  - Were any old freestanding buildings torn down? (Many older homes once had freestanding garages, sheds, or carriage houses.)

  - Who owned the house before you? Do you have their contact information?

- *Local library:* Ask a local librarian to help you navigate a search through old newspaper clippings on microfiche or other archival systems.

- *Internet search:* You can often find photos of your house from previous real-estate listings simply by typing your house's address into a search engine and then selecting "Images." If you're lucky, you might even find old articles about your home.

- *Local historical society:* If your town has a historic preservation committee or a historical society, contact them to see what they can tell you about your house.

◇ GOOD LIVING: *Make Changes When Your Life Is Too Much*

As an overachiever in a culture that rewards overachieving, I need to constantly remind myself that being too busy isn't a virtue. Here are three steps you can take when your current life isn't working and you're ready to make a change.

- *Sort your life's priorities into two categories: primary and secondary.* Primary priorities can include things like maintaining spiritual health, investing in relationships, and making enough money to pay bills. Secondary priorities can include things like saving for retirement, taking vacations, or expanding your business. In that season with young children, my top priorities were (1) spending time with Dale and the children, (2) meeting my commitments to current clients, and (3) attending a weekly women's Bible study.

- *Choose which secondary priorities to put on pause.* Remember, you're not cutting these things out permanently. You're just setting them aside while you restructure your life. When I finally said no to an overpacked life, I knew which secondary priority had to go—expanding my business—so I put a pause on taking on new clients and focused solely on serving my existing clients.

- *Create new income sources, if needed.* I needed to replace the lost income that would have come from signing new clients. Renting rooms to international college students augmented our income while allowing me to focus more on my roles as a wife and a mom.

When you look at your list of secondary priorities, which one(s) can be put on pause? Will you need to replace some lost income in this season? If so, do it in a way that gives your primary priorities the focus they deserve.

It takes humility, creativity, and a little courage to make big changes when life is out of control. Change isn't always convenient, but the rewards are worth the effort. New seasons will come, and when they do, you'll have more time and energy to invest in the secondary priorities you set aside today.

*New seasons
will come,
and you'll have
more time and
energy to invest
in those priorities
you set aside
for today.*

Chapter 5

KITCHEN-CENTRIC

With the exterior of the Lathrop house under renovation, the kitchen remodel was my next priority.

For me, the kitchen is the heart of the home. It's where meals are prepared and often eaten. It's where friends gather and kids do homework. Some of life's richest moments and most lasting memories take place in the kitchen, and it's worth an investment of time and energy to design it well.

The kitchen at the Lathrop house needed that kind of investment. I started imagining what it could become, scouring aisles of local libraries and reading everything I could find on home design—especially kitchens. Nothing I saw in those books and design magazines excited me.

Then I stumbled across the magazine section of a large bookstore, and its European design magazines caught my eye. As I flipped through

When the kitchen began falling apart two weeks after move-in, we discovered it was time for a remodel.

Some of life's richest moments and most lasting memories take place in the kitchen.

---

them, I knew I'd found what I was looking for. I bought the magazines and headed home.

That evening I pored over the photos on those pages, and ideas began to spark. I purchased a magnifying lens so I could see every tiny detail more clearly. These British kitchens were distinct from anything in the US, especially when it came to cabinetry. The doors and drawers in flush-inset cabinets close into the cabinet's face frame (front surface), as they would in a chest of drawers or another piece of fine furniture. That was the look I wanted in our Lathrop kitchen.

I found a set of French doors in the Lathrop dining room that I could repurpose as pantry doors in the kitchen. They would give it an old-world aesthetic and save me the expense of buying a set of new doors.

For a family with young children, there is never a perfect time to remodel a kitchen, but circumstances forced our hand. Within a span of two weeks, both the refrigerator and the dishwasher died. Then, while we were out, a babysitter turned on the kitchen faucet and the handle blew off. Water sprayed everywhere, and she couldn't turn it off. She called us and we raced home. Dale turned off the water main while I mopped up the water. After a bit of investigating, Dale discovered that the broken faucet couldn't be repaired because the faucet, sink, and countertop were all one unit, and everything was so old that replacement parts were no longer available.

The kitchen was falling apart around us. The time to replace all of it was *now*.

I wanted flush-inset cabinetry, but the only manufacturers who sold cabinets like the ones in those European design magazines were in Europe. That wasn't going to work.

If I couldn't buy the cabinets, I'd have to find someone who could build them instead.

BRITISH KITCHEN

Amish carpenters have a reputation for the high quality of their wood-working products, and many produce beautiful custom cabinets. I wondered if we could find an Amish cabinetmaker to build flush-inset cabinets for us. A friend gave us the name and address of an Amish woodworker he knew.

Because the Amish community avoids the use of electronic devices such as telephones and computers, it can be tricky to contact them in any way besides face-to-face communication.

So road trip it was. Dale and I drove the three hours to the shop and talked with the owner. I showed him my magazine photos and sketches, and then explained what I wanted.

"Sorry," he said. "Flush-inset cabinetry requires a level of precision we can't guarantee. Let me give you the name of another cabinetmaker who might be able to help."

He handed us the name of an Amish cabinet shop down the road a few miles. When we arrived, we got another negative response, but this carpenter gave us the name of someone else to try.

We spent the rest of the day leapfrogging our way across the Midwest countryside, from one Amish cabinet business to the next.

"Can't do it," they said, "Too time consuming. Too detailed. No margin of error."

Then we pulled up to our seventh woodworking shop of the day. We parked in front of a large barn labeled "Shop," and a young Amish man stepped outside to greet us. Dressed in traditional black pants, suspenders, a blue handmade shirt, and a broad-brimmed hat, and sporting a beard with no mustache, he smiled and extended his hand.

"Hello!" he said. "I'm Willard Yoder, owner of Yoder Cabinetry. Come inside!" He ushered us in.[1]

Gaslights cast a dim, warm light throughout the entire shop, which held a respectable assortment of quality woodworking tools and saws. Neat stacks

---

[1] Because the Amish community values humility and shuns self-promotion, my cabinetmaker has asked that I not use his real name. Willard Yoder is a pseudonym, and Yoder Cabinetry is not the real name of the business. The names of his cousin and wife (Eli and Leanna) a few paragraphs down are also pseudonyms.

of wood lined the side walls, and cabinets in mid-construction were nestled in groups against the back. The air smelled of wood stain and solvent.

"How can I help you today?" Willard asked.

I handed him my sketches and photos, then began my pitch.

He listened carefully and shook his head. "I don't know anyone who makes flush-inset cabinets," he said.

I laughed. "Tell me about it! We've been denied all day! Do you think you could build these?"

"Well, there are only three of us—my cousin Eli; my wife, Leanna; and me." Sizing up my drawings, he added, "It would be a challenge, but I love custom work. I think we can do this."

That was my humble introduction to the man who would be my cabinet-maker for the next three decades.

Eli, Willard's production manager, walked me through their construction process, detailing the measurements I'd need to provide and the decisions I'd need to make for this order. I promised to return with the finalized plans as soon as possible.

I was eager to move in a completely different direction from the current trend in US kitchens. Not only was the cabinetry style "overlay" (where the doors and drawers close on top of the face frame), but most cabinet doors had raised panels, and all cabinets had the same finish so that everything matched. Plus, those cabinets lined every square inch of wall space. There was zero breathing room.

Matching isn't the way design is done in any other room in a house. In our living rooms, family rooms, and bedrooms, we collect pieces over time. It's a mixture of old and new, a combination of different woods, textures, and colors. Those rooms tell a story, and if any room has stories to be told, it should be the kitchen.

The British kitchens I'd studied in my magazines looked as if they'd been collected carefully over time. Cabinet materials were often mixed, with some pieces painted and some stained wood. Freestanding pieces called "dish dressers" held the family's place settings. Armoires ("larders") held pantry items.

I also noticed their quality. Even from the photos, it was clear that each drawer, door, and handle was well constructed and beautifully finished.

Back at my drafting table, I began drafting a kitchen that was classic, not trendy. I thought of Grandpa Bradbury and his advice to choose classic items that won't go out of style.

I meticulously sketched every detail of the cabinetry. Studying the photos of British kitchens with my magnifying glass, I replicated the proportions and details as accurately as possible, then indicated specific dimensions for each cabinet part. I made sure I got each element correct. We couldn't afford a kitchen island yet, but a dining table we'd inherited from my parents would fit perfectly in that space, so I sketched it in.

Once every detail of my future kitchen was captured and drawn to scale, I scheduled a trip back to the cabinet shop to sit down with Willard and Eli. I showed them the plans I'd drawn, and we talked through every cabinet, confirming the dimensions and details.

As they explained the intricacies of everything from frame construction to creating dovetailed drawer boxes, I took

Our newly renovated, British-inspired kitchen.

note. Talking with those men about my cabinets was my first master-level course in cabinetry design and construction. I was being apprenticed by true artisans of the craft.

This would be the first of many similar conversations, as my business would expand to include complete kitchen designs for clients. Over the next thirty years, I would travel to Willard's shop for such conversations again and again, then drive home with my head filled with new information, eager to apply that knowledge.

When the kids were eight, six, and three, Dale and I welcomed our fourth baby, Dan, into the Stoffer gang. He was our grand finale.

I was ready to savor this last season of babyhood and prepare to embrace whatever new seasons were yet to come.

It took us many years to complete the remodel of the Lathrop house, but we eventually finished the attic and built an addition that gave us more living space for our active family. In the end, the home had six bedrooms—and three and a half bathrooms! True to the contract Dale had asked me to sign when we moved in, when the last room was finished, I didn't even ask about moving to a new house.

FIRST DESIGN

Jean Stoffer Interiors was now nine years old, and even with my intentionally slower pace since Grace had been born, my previous clients were spreading the word, and my phone kept ringing. When Dan was a few months old, I got a call from Judy, a former client.

The whole family welcomes baby Daniel— the grand finale for the Stoffer gang.

"Jean, we're building a custom home," she said. "Jim and I bought a site in a new development in north River Forest, and we'd like to talk to you about designing our kitchen."

I knew the area. The vacant land had belonged to the Dominican Priory, and they'd begun selling it off for custom homes. This was exciting news for our town since every lot had already been developed and no new homes had been built since the 1950s.

River Forest is an architecturally rich village, filled with one-of-a-kind, prewar houses. In keeping with this history, the new development would be constructed entirely of unique custom homes.

"Ever since I saw your kitchen, I can't stop thinking about it," Judy said. "It's like nothing I've found in any magazine or design book. It's fully modern in function, but it looks more . . . collected, as if there's a history to the place. That's exactly what Jim and I want for our kitchen."

Judy wasn't the first person to make these kinds of comments when they saw my kitchen on Lathrop. Evidently I was developing a certain design aesthetic that was appealing to other people, too.

"So what do you think?" she asked.

"This sounds fantastic!" I said. And I meant it.

Kitchen design was a different beast from the interior decorating I'd focused on in previous projects. It was the early 1990s, and with the internet in its infancy, every item for an interior decorating project—from wallpaper samples to countertops to decor to carpeting options—had to be sourced from local showrooms. It meant driving from showroom to showroom—not a work-from-home job.

Designing kitchens, on the other hand, is primarily about drawing. It's about working on layouts and elevations. The vast majority of design work could be done from my drafting table at home. With four kids under nine, I could take on this type of project without missing out on my kids' childhoods. And the idea of designing a kitchen from scratch fascinated me.

This would be my first custom kitchen design for a client. In Judy and Jim's home—an English-inspired cottage style—I'd lay out the whole space, determine where appliances and plumbing would go, and design custom cabinetry in the British style I loved—and Jim and Judy did too.

The next day, with tape measure in hand and Dan in an infant carrier, I met Judy at the building site. I took notes as she explained her vision for the space, and then I measured everything.

I dove into Jim and Judy's project with intention. During naptimes, I sketched and erased until I came up with a design I was eager to show them.

It had been a couple of years since Willard had built my British-style cabinets for Lathrop. I wrote to him and said, "Remember me? I've got another kitchen I'd like you to build!"

Willard was all in. As soon as Jim and Judy signed off on the plans, I mailed them to Willard. My second British-inspired kitchen was officially underway.

When the house was finished, the kitchen had the exact European countryside vibe Jim and Judy were looking for: a room that looked like it had evolved over time with collected pieces. It was warm and cozy, with a soul. I nominated it to be part of an annual kitchen walk fundraiser for a local charity. Each year ten newly remodeled kitchens were chosen to be featured, and I was honored when Judy and Jim's kitchen was selected to be part of the walk.

The day before the tour, I styled the kitchen with fresh fruits and vegetables,

The Amish-made, flushed-inset cabinets looked fantastic in Jim and Judy's kitchen.

flowers, and loaves of fresh-baked artisan bread. Looking around the room, I felt as if I could be standing in the kitchen of a true English cottage. It was beautiful—and was distinct from any of the other kitchens on the walk.

The day of the walk, a line formed outside Judy and Jim's house because the people inside didn't want to leave. I stayed in the kitchen all day, answering questions from everyone who came through.

When I got home that night, I was on a high, talking Dale's ear off about every aspect of the experience.

"I knew it went well because our answering machine was buzzing all day," Dale said. "You've already gotten voice messages from prospective clients."

"Designing kitchens is way more fun than decorating interiors," I said. "I want to do more projects like this—maybe two or three kitchens a year."

It was now 1995 and I'd been doing interior decorating for more than a decade. If I wanted to change the focus of my business, I decided it was time to change my business name, too. I made the shift from Jean Stoffer Interiors to Jean Stoffer Design, a subtle but substantial difference. Moving forward, my focus would be on designing custom kitchens.

GOOD BUSINESS: *Become an Expert*

When I was starting out in design, I said yes to anything and everything. But once I began to focus solely on kitchens, I studied kitchens in great depth. With all my experience in one specific area, I developed a strong knowledge base, and people felt relieved and confident about hiring a kitchen design professional.

No matter your line of work, you'll do well to choose a focused area and specialize in it. Learning something deeply allows you to become a sought-after expert, and you'll never regret learning more about something that interests you.

Ask yourself these questions to narrow your focus, become an expert, and increase your business.

1. *What are you uniquely qualified to provide?* Do you offer a skill or product that few others offer? If so, promote that part of your business.

2. *What gap in the market can you fill?* Do clients often comment about a particular aspect of your business they can't seem to find elsewhere? Make it your goal to become known as the go-to person for that.

3. *What aspect of your business gives you the greatest joy?* People excel at things they're passionate about. Make your business more enjoyable by specializing in what's rewarding for you.

Chapter 6

GROWING PAINS

Shortly after finishing Jim and Judy's kitchen, I got a call from a potential new client. The couple who bought two lots next to Jim and Judy had seen their kitchen and were interested in bringing that type of design into their new build.

I met the owners at their current home, and they rolled out the plans for their new house.

"We'd like you to design the kitchen, baths, laundry room, butler's pantry, library–basically every room that has cabinetry," they said.

This was a big opportunity and an even bigger challenge–one I was eager to accept. I knew from Jim and Judy's project that I could do most of the work from home during naps and school. I now had margin to begin saying yes to new clients–and so I did just that.

I was well into working on the designs when the couple called. "We're signing a contract to allow our house to be the ASID showcase house. Are you familiar with ASID?"

I was definitely familiar! The American Society of Interior Designers (ASID) is the professional association that represents all aspects of design. Each room in the showcase house would be designed by a different design professional, and all designs would be okayed by a high-profile interior designer called the chairperson of the show house.

I would be interfacing with at least a dozen professionally educated designers. My design training included half of a drafting class at a junior college, so I didn't even qualify to apply for membership with ASID, yet my cabinetry designs would be all over that house. Did I feel slightly out of my league? Yes. Was I excited? *Absolutely.*

Several months later, with the designs finished and installed, I got a phone call from the showcase house's PR and graphic design coordinator, who was in charge of creating the printed guidebook that the tour's 10,000 guests would reference as they walked through the home.

Taking out a full-page ASID ad was a big risk—but well worth it.

"Jean, your work is fantastic," she said. "You really should take out an ad in the guidebook with professional photographs. These people on the tour are your future clients—don't miss this opportunity! I'm cheering for you."

Because it was the pre-internet 1990s, the guidebook would be people's sole gateway to contacting designers. This was new territory for me. Word of mouth had worked fine at attracting new clients thus far. Should I spend good money on advertising? How expensive would a professional photographer be? Did I want the business to grow bigger?

Yes. Let's see what Jean Stoffer Design can become, I decided. I scheduled a photographer and placed a full-page ad on the inside front cover.

When the guidebook came out, I got an early copy and flipped through its pages. My ad looked terrific. I turned to the rooms that featured my cabinetry. Each spread featured photographs, a sketch, and a list of contributors. Jean Stoffer Design was listed as the cabinetry designer. Local press covered the show house, which meant more publicity.

As a result of that show house project, new clients found out about me, fell in love with the welcoming feel of a classic British kitchen, and hired me to design kitchens in their homes. Thanks to the charity kitchen walk and the ASID show house design tour, I locked into my area of design expertise: custom kitchens, the heart of the home. I worked on honing my craft and committed myself to doing quality work every time.

That next year I designed six kitchens.

Keeping a steady stream of kitchen-design projects coming in and designing them while my kids were in school or sleeping became my rhythm over the next several years. The nature of my business meant that at any given time I was working on several different projects at once, all in different stages of design and installation.

Despite the busyness, my heart was full, my pace somewhat sane, and my days filled with things that gave me joy. I loved designing. I loved partnering with my clients to dream up kitchens that would meet the needs of their families. I loved meeting the needs of my own family. I loved it all.

ANCHORS

Despite loving my busy life and having the support of a husband who cheered me on, I needed girlfriends. Early on in River Forest, I'd developed friendships with a group of women I met at church. Most of them had stepped away from corporate jobs in downtown Chicago when they had kids. Now they were stay-at-home moms.

I'd never been a career woman in a Chicago high-rise; I'd only worked from home at my small business. So when I started having children, I didn't have such a stark choice to make—I simply worked in moderation while the kids were little—but I identified completely with those moms. They became my anchors, the people I turned to when I felt overwhelmed or made mistakes as a mom. We encouraged each other and shared practical ideas about how to manage it all.

Every woman needs a friend who shares her values, supports her decisions, offers wisdom when needed, and is there to laugh and cry with.

Having a dear friend like Jill enriches my life, then and now.

Spending time with my good friend Jill was one of the ways I refueled myself. We took regular walks together and talked the entire time. I'm sure we got more of a cardio workout from the talking than the walking. Every woman needs a friend who shares her values, supports her decisions, offers wisdom when needed, and is there to laugh and cry with. For me, that was Jill.

BOOK OF BUSINESS

My cabinetmaker, Willard, continued to build the top-quality flush-inset cabinets I designed for my custom kitchen clients. For every new order, I would leave my house at 4 a.m. to be at his shop when it opened at 7 a.m. I'd work with the production manager until about 11:30 a.m., then head home, arriving in time for school to let out.

One day when I was at the shop to discuss some cabinetry plans with Eli, Willard called me over.

"Jean, I've been working with a developer/builder in the western suburbs of Chicago for a long time. He's building a hundred homes in a new subdivision, and we're designing and building the cabinetry for all those homes."

"Yes, I've seen those cabinets when I come to place orders," I said. "That's a lot of work!"

"It's running me ragged," he said. "I've been going back and forth to Chicago—sometimes two or three times a week—and it's just too much. I'd like to find a way to keep the business but reduce my involvement on the design and customer service side."

"What do you have in mind?" I asked.

"I want you to consider taking this work, Jean," he said. "I don't want to hand this off to just anyone, and I know you could handle this level of design."

I was stunned. "You're talking about the whole development?" I asked.

"Yes. I would like you to consider handling this book of business," he said.

Whoa. More than one hundred houses! I started doing the math in my head. My heart leaped.

I needed time to think. Dan was now three years old, and Grace was not yet six. John and David were in elementary school. This business would dramatically increase my revenue—and dramatically increase the hours I would be working. I needed time to pray about a decision of this magnitude.

"Can I get back to you?" I asked. "I'm flattered you think I can handle this, but I need to think about it and talk to Dale."

"Yes, of course," he agreed. "Talk it over and let me know."

I drove home deep in thought. *Father, is this something you want me to say yes to?*

The next morning, as is my habit, I poured myself a cup of coffee and sat down to begin my quiet time with God. On most days—not every day, but most—I spend time reading Scripture. I find that the Bible provides wisdom and perspective for my life, and it often speaks to my current situation. For me, reading Scripture is like reading a personal letter from God.

On that particular day, I opened my Bible to the place I'd left off the day before—the story of Abram and his nephew Lot in the book of Genesis (chapter 13). It's a story I'd known since childhood, but that day the story shed new meaning.

Abram was following God's guidance to reach a chosen land. He'd left his own region of Haran (in modern-day Turkey) with his wife, Sarai, and his grown nephew Lot. Abram and Sarai had no children of their own at that point, and Lot was like a son to them.

They arrived together in the Promised Land (in modern-day Israel), where they flourished. But over time Abram and Lot's flocks and herds grew to be more than the land could sustain. They had too much business for one area. Abram suggested they go separate ways, and he gave Lot first choice of the available land.

Lot chose the lush, fertile Jordan River valley to the east, so Abram headed west toward Canaan, where the land looked less conducive to farming and raising herds of livestock. Then God extended the ultimate blessing to Abram—the promise that his offspring would be as plentiful as the dust of the earth, from generation to generation.

At the end of the day, my family was—and is—my highest priority.

Despite Abram's generosity and kindness, Lot's family didn't thrive in the Jordan River valley. They had abundant riches—flocks, herds, crops—but they became relationally and spiritually bankrupt. Apart from Abram's wise influence, they went adrift. The following chapters of Genesis tell about Lot and his family moving to Sodom (of Sodom and Gomorrah fame) and Abram eventually rescuing him from the destruction of those evil cities.

Meanwhile, on land that had far less potential, Abram thrived. God eventually gave him and his wife, Sarai, a son, and he became known as the father of many nations.

Lot leaped at the chance to grow his business by seizing the best pastures for himself. But it didn't turn out well for his family. They had all the resources they needed, but their relationships suffered.

When Abram surrendered the best land to his nephew, he had no idea if he could be successful in Canaan. In putting his nephew first, he chose a harder path, a less sure opportunity. He and his wife settled in Canaan and stayed connected to God. They were obedient to God's guidance, and they thrived.

As I read my Bible, I was struck by the similarities between my situation and Lot's. It was as if God were using this story to speak to me. I had a clear choice: Would I choose an opportunity to vastly increase my business at the potential expense of my family?

No. I would not make that choice. I would not choose resources over relationships. I would not bury myself under the load of designing countless kitchens for other families while my three-year-old wondered why his mother was always at her drafting table, unavailable to him.

It was an important decision. Designing an entire development would have catapulted my fledgling business to the next level. By saying no to Willard, I was saying yes to growing my business slowly, one project at a time. Would I ever see an opportunity like that again? I had no idea.

But one thing I knew: God had already given me an opportunity that was mine alone—the privilege of being my kids' mom. I would not squander that privilege. Whatever the future held for my business, I would do my best to make one right decision at a time.

I wrote Willard a letter, thanking him for his generous offer. Then I turned it down.

GOOD LIVING: *Make Value-Based Decisions*

What I've learned in the decades since turning down that business is that God knows everything I need, and he cares deeply about me. My first priority was my family, and my decisions flowed from that value. I could confidently say no to an opportunity today because I knew God would take care of us in the future.

If you are facing an important decision, you can use these three decision-making steps to help you determine what you value most.

1. *Get clear on your priorities.* Your life likely contains lots of good things, but which ones are most important right now? Consider all those priorities—family, kids, relationships, spiritual life, fitness, profit, employees, creativity, generosity, etc.—and decide which will be your top three values in this season.

2. *Evaluate how a decision will affect your values.* Will this benefit your family relationships? Foster creativity? Benefit your employees? Allow for generosity? Increase profit?

3. *Make your decision based on top values.* Trust that other opportunities will come your way as long as you keep making decisions that support who you are and what you value.

GOOD DESIGN: *Find Design Inspiration*

There are a million different places to be inspired when it comes to design. Here are my top five sources when I'm in need of information and inspiration.

1. *Walk through neighborhoods with good architecture.* Take photos of homes that inspire you.

2. *Tour well-designed homes.* Attend a local home tour or a real-estate open house that features a design style you love.

3. *Read international design magazines.* Check out your local library or large bookstore for these gems.

4. *Study the interiors of gorgeous homes in television shows or movies.* Watch a series like *The Crown* or *Downton Abbey* and observe the architecture and decor from bygone eras.

5. *Study classic design.* The book I keep by my side while designing is *Get Your House Right: Architectural Elements to Use and Avoid* by Marianne Cusato and Ben Pentreath.

*God had
given me an
opportunity
that was
mine alone—
the privilege
of being
my kids' mom.*

Chapter 7

STEPPING OUT

Every parent knows that raising young children is physically exhausting, but as our family grew older, I discovered that raising teens is also a workout—an emotional one. There's no shortcut for the sheer investment of time and mental fortitude it takes to guide kids into adulthood.

One of my biggest hopes for each of my children was that they would come to know God in a personal way. I enjoyed weaving God into our conversations at home, and I wanted them to discover for themselves that he is faithful, worthy of their trust, and personally involved in their everyday lives.

Dale and I made the decision early on to enroll our kids in public school. We knew and respected many Christian families who chose private schools or homeschooling for their kids, but we wanted our kids to experience life in its messy fullness while they were still under our roof so they could talk with us about what they saw, read, and were taught.

I was determined to invite God into our daily lives at every opportunity while they were young—and to prep them to choose Christian colleges later in life. That way, the friends (and possible spouses) they met in college as semi-formed young adults would likely be people with similar worldviews who could encourage them in their faith.

I would often tell them, "You can choose any college you want, but if you'd like help paying for it, it must be a Christian school." Solid plan, right?

Any parent with more than one child can tell you that each kid is unique. Same gene pool; entirely different personalities. This couldn't have been truer with David, John, Grace, and Dan.

David was full of energy, confidence, and a little mischief. John was agreeable and personable, and had a creative bent from an early age. Grace was an inquisitive innovator, always the first with a new idea or fresh insight. And Dan was chill, quiet, and very others focused, never holding a grudge. They were typical siblings who either loved playing together or drove each other crazy, depending on the day—or hour or minute. Some days certain combinations of kids and parents worked together wonderfully. Other days, not so much.

David was a natural leader. He needed to figure things out for himself. Even as a young child, he struggled to take anyone's word for something—including his parents'. He often took charge, and his wiring was a little like my own, so I tracked with him easily. But David and Dale, whose personalities were quite different, were like fire and ice.

There's no shortcut for the sheer investment of time it takes to guide kids into adulthood.

When tempers flared, I would jump in and try to smooth things out, taking on the role of Switzerland between two warring parties—a role no one asked me to play, mind you.

"Can't you just obey without arguing?" I would ask David after a fray with his dad.

"Why do you have to be so aggressive with him?" I would ask Dale later.

It was exhausting trying to be the neutral party. I was trying to help, but it only made matters worse. It would take me many more years to understand how my interference got in the way of David and Dale developing their own way of working things out.

NOTES OF SOUL CARE

When both parenting and work demand our full attention, something has to give. During those intense years, I moved many of my personal interests or hobbies to the back burner—a temporary self-denial that was worth it as I invested in raising my kids.

One thing I wasn't willing to put on the back burner was my relationship with God. I took time to care for my soul, making sure my heart was in the right place.

For me, music is a spiritual pathway that fills me and helps me connect with God. When I'd taken piano lessons all through my childhood, playing hymns and worship songs had brought pure joy. I missed those times at the keyboard, and I longed for a piano of my own.

After much searching through want ads, I came across a used grand piano in my price range and decided to take a look.

When I arrived at the seller's studio, I saw that the old instrument had endured decades of neglect. Its black finish was scratched and worn. The ivory keys were chipped, and several were missing. I played a few notes, wincing at how sorely out of tune it was, but the tone itself held promise. The piano had good bones, and I could see its potential.

High-quality grand pianos are five- or six-figure instruments when purchased new, but this long-neglected beauty was only $750. I bought it and arranged to have it delivered.

Even though it was out of tune, I loved it. I would often play one handed, bouncing a baby on my left knee and playing with my right hand. My time with that piano became a form of soul care.

Still, the condition of the neglected instrument bothered me. I repeatedly hired a piano tuner to come out and tune it, but it simply could not hold a tune. Everything was worn out and broken. It needed a gut remodel.

My old piano teacher's son owned a piano restoration business, so I asked him to take a look. He recognized my piano's hidden beauty, and he spent six months restoring it. He refinished the wood and replaced the pinboard, rusted strings, broken keys, and hammers.

At long last, my restored piano returned home, and we set it up in the living room. Dale was out of town the day it was delivered, and I had a few minutes to play before the kids got home from school.

I put my hands on the keys, closed my eyes, and began playing my favorite hymn. "Amazing grace, how sweet the sound . . ."

My eyes filled just as John walked in.

"Whoa! The piano!" he said. "What's wrong?"

I swallowed the lump in my throat. "It's just—perfect. It sounds so good. The tone is so rich and warm. Can you hear it?"

The timbre of the notes coming from this refurbished instrument was like nothing I'd ever heard. As a child I'd learned to play on a brand-new upright my dad had bought for us girls. It was a high-quality instrument, but my used grand had been built in the 1920s and its wood case had seasoned over the decades. The reverberation of the wood had a warmth to it that comes only with age and time.

I closed my eyes and continued playing. *Thank you, God. What a gift!*

Hearing the difference in the piano's sound before and after restoration gave me new appreciation for the old homes I'd worked on in recent years. Something can become better with age—even better than new—when it's placed in loving hands with the right skills for the task.

SUB-ZERO AND WOLF CONTEST

As Jean Stoffer Design slowly expanded and I took on bigger projects, any mistakes I made became more expensive. Obviously, a client shouldn't pay for my errors, so when cabinets, fixtures, or materials were ordered incorrectly, I would eat the cost. That meant I ended up owning a lot of nice things I hadn't planned on purchasing! How I missed the days when a quick stroke of my eraser could fix a mistake.

One time I ordered a custom, high-end executive desk and credenza for a client's office, but when the set arrived at their house, it was in the wrong stain color, and it looked horrible. These were pieces I'd designed from scratch, so they weren't returnable. I reordered them, double-checking that I chose the correct stain color.

All was not lost. We put the unreturnable furniture to good use in Dale's office, but it was still a costly mistake. It heightened my attention to detail on future orders, since our budget couldn't sustain these types of wasted expenses.

As projects grew more complicated, I began to follow the work of some incredible designers even more closely. At the top of my list of design heroes was Mick De Giulio, who's been designing kitchens—and earning recognition for his skill—for decades. His designs are layered, collected, and engineered to an elite level. I was a huge De Giulio fan. Even though we'd never met, Mick was my mentor, and I was his anonymous pupil.

Like many industries, the kitchen-design community rewards success by holding competitions. One such contest was the Kitchen Design Contest held by Sub-Zero and Wolf, manufacturers of high-end refrigeration and cooking appliances.[2] Held every two years, the contest attracted entrants from around the world. Regional winners were invited to the celebration at a fancy resort in Scottsdale, Arizona, that year, where three finalists were chosen by judges who were all luminaries in the world of architecture and design.

"I'm going to enter this contest," I told Dale.

"What's our prize when you win?" my biggest fan asked.

"Don't get your hopes up," I cautioned. "It's a long shot. Hundreds of experienced designers from around the world submit entries, and the judges only choose three finalists from the Midwest region. Chicago's an architectural mecca, so our region is packed with amazingly gifted designers and architects. But why not try?"

"You can't win if you don't enter," he said. "You're new, but you're not inexperienced. You must have twenty projects under your belt already."

"Twenty-seven, actually," I corrected. "Twenty-seven kitchens."

I knew which kitchen to enter. I had recently completed a kitchen remodel in a 1902 home, and the owner had asked me to create a period reproduction of a 1937 kitchen.

"That's pretty specific," I told her. But she was in the process of having a 1937 woodburning cooking stove converted to natural gas, and that stove would be the focal point of the design. So I did some research and got creative.

We covered the ceiling with tin tiles from the period and installed a

---

[2] Sub-Zero and Wolf now includes Cove dishwashing appliances as well.

freestanding porcelain farm sink from an architectural salvage lot. I designed the cabinets by replicating the original cabinetry I'd found in the butler's pantry, and we salvaged antique wavy glass to put in the upper cabinet doors. The client finished the fir cabinets onsite using shellac, an outdated finish used during that period. When we were done, it looked like a brand-new 1937 kitchen. She loved it—and so did I.

I took pictures of her kitchen using my 35mm Canon and my limited photography skills. I stayed up late the night before the entry had to be postmarked, making sure every entry detail was checked off. Then I placed the entry in the mail and waited.

Three months later, I got a phone call.

"Hi, Jean." It was a voice I didn't recognize. "I'm calling from Sub-Zero and Wolf's Kitchen Design Contest, and congratulations! Your submission has been selected as one of the three finalists in your region, and one of forty regional finalists overall!"

A regional finalist! Unbelievable!

"This year's contest drew more than eight hundred submissions, so being selected is quite an accomplishment," she continued. "Sub-Zero and Wolf will fly you and a companion to Scottsdale, Arizona, where you'll be our guests at the Gainey Ranch resort. Our panel of judges will announce three global winners at a formal gala."

The woman and I talked for a few more minutes while I jotted down all the details.

When Dale got home from work, I greeted him at the door. "My design is a regional finalist!" I said. "All the finalists get an all-expenses-paid vacation for two in Scottsdale!"

"Congratulations!" he said, hugging me. "I'm so proud of you. I knew you could do it. And . . . um . . . can I be your plus-one?"

Being chosen as a regional finalist was a shock. I had no illusions that my kitchen project would be selected as one of the three global winners, but the opportunity to meet some of my design heroes at the celebration or chat with them at one of the activities we could participate in (hot-air ballooning!) would be the best prize of all. The free vacation in Arizona was icing on the cake. Dale and I hadn't taken a real vacation with just the two of us in years.

My first entry for Sub-Zero and Wolf's Kitchen Design Contest: a reproduction of a 1937 kitchen.

That fall we flew to beautiful Arizona. A limo picked us up at the airport, and Dale and I spent the short drive to Scottsdale enjoying the mini fridge, snacks, champagne, and TV/DVD-player combo (which was cutting edge for the day). I couldn't believe we were riding in a real limo!

When we pulled into the resort, a valet helped us out of the car and summoned a bellhop to help with our luggage.

"Wow, fancy!" I whispered.

We'd never stayed at a place this nice. With four kids in tow, we were masters at vacations on the cheap—usually driving cross-country in our Suburban and staying with Dale's parents. (*Bless them, Lord. We were not easy guests!*)

Our hotel room was gorgeous, and the luxurious bathroom was stocked with high-end beauty products I never splurged on back home. "Go easy on the shampoo, Dale," I said. "I want to bring the little bottle home."

A gift basket filled with fresh fruit and chocolate sat on the small dining table. *How did they know I love chocolate?* A bottle of champagne was chilling on ice.

Dale popped the cork and poured each of us a glass.

"How do you think things are going at home with my parents and the kids?" I asked.

"I seriously do not care," Dale said, and then, raising his glass, he added, "To us."

"To us," I said, clinking my glass with his. "My favorite team."

At the formal gala the next night, Dale and I dressed the part. I'd bought a new dress for the occasion, and Dale wore a white linen sport coat. Walking into the ballroom, we felt very fancy.

After hors d'oeuvres and drinks, we looked for our name cards among beautifully appointed tables and took our seats. Jim Bakke, CEO of Sub-Zero and Wolf, took the stage.

"Welcome, and congratulations to each of you regional finalists," he said. "Your work is brilliant, and we're honored to recognize you."

He then introduced the panel of judges, and I was starstruck. I recognized every single name. They were designers whose work I followed, studied, and respected.

The host announced the top three global winners, and I cheered for each one. I knew what it took to win at this level of competition, and each design was truly inspiring.

For me, the real fun began after the gala, when the judges and designers mingled and chatted.

I spotted my favorite designer, Mick De Giulio, across the room. I pulled Dale over. "Look, it's Mick! Mick De Giulio!" I said. "Let's go meet him!"

Mick was a fellow finalist from the Midwest region that year. He'd been designing kitchens for decades, and I'm sure he'd been to lots of similar events and won many awards. When I introduced myself, he was warm and gracious.

"I loved your kitchen, Jean," he said. "The detail was extraordinary. Well done. There's always tough competition in our region. You should feel really great about your win."

He had taken the time to learn about my kitchen.

"Thank you," I said. "You couldn't possibly know this, but I have been studying your work for years, and in a sense, you have apprenticed me from afar. I am inspired by your designs and your attention to detail. Your work is innovative but not trendy. I just wanted to thank you."

"Wow, thank you, Jean," he said. "I've had many brilliant people around me who've inspired me. I'm honored you are inspired by my work. Keep going! Keep expanding your ideas. I'm cheering you on."

Mick De Giulio isn't exactly a household name. He isn't famous beyond the kitchen-design community. But he is a true innovator, and I took note that even though he worked on projects with budgets twenty times bigger than mine, he had taken the time to chat with me and encourage me.

THE COTSWOLDS

"Want to go to England with me?" Jill asked over coffee one afternoon.

"What?" I asked. Jill often traveled internationally for Opportunity International (OI), an organization she volunteered with. She often stayed extra days before or after these trips, and until now I'd always said no to her invitations to join her. But England? *Hmm. I may have to think about this one.*

"I'm attending an OI board meeting in Oxford," she continued. "I'd love to tack on a few days to explore London and the Cotswolds. Come with me! I know you've never traveled internationally before, but I heard a rumor that they speak English in England, so this could be a great intro trip for you. We'll do it together!"

My initial reaction to any leisure that would take me away from work and family was to say no. Dale had no interest in traveling outside the US, and the whole concept seemed overwhelming to me. But for some reason, I allowed myself to consider Jill's invitation this time.

"How long are you thinking?" I asked.

"Let's stay a week to make it worth your trouble," she said. "I'll take good care of you. I really think you'll love it!"

"I'll think about it," I said. "And I need to talk to Dale."

Dale doesn't like it when I'm gone. I knew he could hold down the fort, but he wouldn't be thrilled with my being in England for a week. This would be a big ask.

We discussed it at length, and in the end, he said, "You should go. I can handle things at home."

I was shocked—this was a huge moment for us. I bought my plane tickets before he could change his mind and waited for Jill to tell me what to do next.

Jill and me biking our way through the Cotswolds.

About a week before we left, Jill finalized the plans for our trip.

"I found a company that offers self-guided bike tours through the lush, green landscape of the Cotswolds. We'll set our own pace, and we'll stay in bed-and-breakfasts in rural villages along the way. The company will provide the bikes and move our luggage to the next B and B each day. I know you'll love it!"

Jill was right. I was on cloud nine from start to finish. We cycled our way across the green countryside, stopping in local villages whenever we felt like it. We stayed at local inns and ate in local pubs. We stopped by quaint cottages and poked our heads into tiny shops. I took photos of everything.

I was completely enthralled by the Cotswold Hills. It turned out that riding a bike was the best way to experience a new place. We moved along at a nice pace, fast enough to reach our destination each night, but slow enough to see, smell, feel, and hear the outdoors. We could stop whenever and wherever we wanted, exploring formal English gardens, sprawling lavender fields, and ancient homes along the way. I popped my head into genuine British kitchens wherever we went.

My world was enlarged on that trip. The experience solidified my design aesthetic, and I came home rejuvenated and inspired. I couldn't wait to get back to my drafting table and begin applying some of what I'd discovered.

SUB-ZERO AND WOLF REVISITED

Prior to leaving for England, I had entered the Sub-Zero and Wolf's Kitchen Design Contest for the third time. I'd been a regional winner the first time I'd entered, but when I entered two years later, my design wasn't selected. This time, the kitchen I submitted highlighted an heirloom of the owner's family—a silver coffee urn.

My submission was chosen as a regional finalist, and Dale and I flew to Scottsdale, where we again stayed at the resort and dressed up for the Friday-night gala.

It had been four years since I'd last attended this event, and by now I knew several of the regional finalists. Our paths had crossed at trade shows or conferences, and I admired their work. It was a joy to mingle with them before dinner and be inspired by their designs.

As dessert was being served, Jim Bakke took the stage and welcomed everyone.

"More than 1,500 designers from around the world submitted entries for this year's contest," he said. "So the fact that only forty of you designers are sitting here means you are already a winner. And now, it's time to announce the entries our judges have deemed the top three best kitchen designs. I'll describe the kitchen's design and then announce the designer's name and company."

"Our third-place kitchen is restrained in its elegance," he began. "At first glance it's simple, but the longer you look, it becomes rich with details. There is beautiful symmetry throughout the space."

Well, lots of entries could be described this way, I thought. *Still, the design he's describing is not not mine . . .*

"This kitchen's finer points include a mixture of lighting fixtures and hardware, and ceiling beams detailed to harmonize with the home's architecture."

Still not not mine . . . Could it be . . . ?

" . . . and the incorporation of a treasured family heirloom: a large silver Italian coffee urn."

Oh my gosh! That's my kitchen!

"Please congratulate our third-place winner, Jean Stoffer of Jean Stoffer Design."

I couldn't believe my ears. The judges had chosen my design as number three in the world. I sat stunned, my jaw hanging open as the audience began to cheer.

"Take the stage, honey," Dale said, standing to pull out my chair.

I hugged him and stepped to the stage, suddenly nervous. The strap on my sandal wouldn't stay on, and I had trouble walking all the way to the front. The judges shook my hand, and the host held out a plaque with my name and *Jean Stoffer Design* engraved on it. As I thanked them, I caught Dale's eye. He sat there clapping, his face filled with pride.

At breakfast the next morning, a regional winner from New York and her photographer husband headed our way and introduced themselves.

"Your designs are not being represented well," the husband said. "Your photographs are clearly not professional. You need pro shots." *I can tell he's a New Yorker. He doesn't mince words.*

He was right. My photos didn't measure up against the photography of all the other entrants.

What an honor to receive my award from Sub-Zero and Wolf president Jim Bakke.

Hiring a professional photographer would cost considerable money, but I was entering a new season. The kids were all in school, and I had more time to focus on the business. I'd already hired a CAD (computer-aided design) draftsperson to transfer my graph-paper sketches into professional-quality electronic designs. That move alone had given me more margin. I was ready to see where this business could go.

I hired the New York photographer to shoot six recent kitchen projects, all of which were placed in home-design magazines and two of which found their way into books on design.

"Mom, you need a website," said John, who was now in high school.

My winning kitchen design's statement piece: a large silver Italian coffee urn.

"Websites aren't just for huge companies anymore. Small businesses are creating websites where people can see their products. You need to get online so people can find you and see your work."

John was right. With professional photos and my own collection of shots, I hired a web designer, who built a simple portfolio website, jeanstofferdesign.com, where people could scroll through past projects, read a little bit about my work, and contact me if they liked my design aesthetic.

The exposure in books and magazines, along with my website, gave potential clients increased confidence that they were selecting someone who could do the job.

Dan was now in late elementary school, Grace was in middle school, and John and David were in high school. I could take on new clients without overly disrupting my family. Dale was still working from home and was very engaged with the kids, especially in their sports and activities.

Parenting teenagers required more relational time than ever, and it helped that our house was a "hub house" for countless events: weekend barbeques, postgame pizza parties, and homecoming photo shoots. It was the hangout place for our kids and their friends.

It gave me joy to see our home filled with conversations and laughter from our kids and their friends. All those years I'd spent remodeling the Lathrop house were paying dividends for our family. The ugliest house in town had turned into a classic, and the memories we were making there were timeless.

⌂ GOOD LIVING: *Prioritize Soul Care*

No matter what roles you play in life, tending to your inner world matters. Soul care—setting aside time to do things that are life giving—replenishes you and keeps you emotionally, spiritually, and relationally centered.

For me, playing the piano is a form of soul care. It's a creative outlet that connects me to God. The time I invest when I sit down to play renews my inner self. I also love going to church. I enjoy singing worship songs, reading Scripture, and listening to teaching from the Bible. The experience leaves me encouraged, inspired, and filled up spiritually for the week.

What nourishes your soul? Maybe it's journaling after you read Scripture, taking a walk and praying with a friend, or listening to worship music while you clean or do laundry. Maybe it's starting your day with a few minutes of solitude or spending time in nature. Whatever it is, make it a priority to set aside time for soul care. For me, engaging in spiritual practices helps me get to know God better, which in turn leads to peace, joy, and a heightened awareness of my purpose in this world.

GOOD LIVING: *Expand Your World*

My trip to the Cotswolds broadened my perspective and exposed me to architecture, geography, people, and design styles I'd previously only read about. It was exhilarating to experience them firsthand.

If international travel isn't possible, load your bike in the car and drive somewhere beautiful. Then explore by bicycle. If you're not a cyclist, consider walking, hiking, or simply setting a slower pace on a road trip. Allow time to stop, smell, listen, see, and taste. Take it all in—and capture it with photos.

Chapter 8

LETTING GO

David had always been a strong-willed kid, and now that he was a senior in high school, things were no different. With his God-given wiring of needing to wrestle things to the ground for himself, he wasn't the type to be handed his parents' faith unquestioned. It should have come as no surprise when he began having spiritual doubts. He needed to either own Christianity for himself or set it aside.

This freaked me out as a mom, and I complained to God in my prayers.

I've been so purposeful all these years, taking every opportunity to show the kids how much you mean to me and how you fit into life, I complained. *Now here we are, with our oldest about to graduate high school, and he's having doubts? No. Not okay. This cannot happen so late in the game!*

GAP YEAR

The year before, we'd taken David to visit Cedarville, a small Christian college in Ohio. He seemed to like it, and in my mind, it was a done deal. David would attend there in the fall.

I wasn't prepared for his casual announcement at breakfast one morning: "I'm not going to Cedarville this fall. Actually, I'm not going anywhere. I think I'll take a gap year instead."

A gap year? What on earth is a gap year? I tried to keep my cool as I felt my carefully calculated plan for David's life slipping from my grasp.

"Gap year, huh?" I asked. "Like, a year off?"

"Yes, exactly," he said. "I'm just not ready to head straight into college, so I'd like to take a year to figure stuff out."

What is there to figure out? You finish high school and then start college. It's not complicated. I tried to remain calm.

"What would you like to do during your gap year?" I asked.

"Not sure. I've got some ideas. I'll probably need a passport."

Lord, help me! He wants to forego college so he can fly across the globe with no real plan. I tried to breathe.

There were still a few months before David graduated—plenty of time for me to pray him back into my plan. And if I couldn't get him to go to college in the fall, I could at least find him the perfect gap-year experience where he'd be safe in a nice Christian bubble.

God was one step ahead of me, as usual.

In the weeks that followed, two things happened. First, my women's group began working our way through a book about control.[3] The week after David dropped his gap-year bombshell, our discussion leader got right to the point.

"Our need to control is rooted in two things," she said. "Fear and pride."

Yikes. Those words struck home. I immediately saw that David's desire for a gap year petrified me because I wanted to control David's spiritual development. I wanted to lock him into becoming a Christ-following adult by sending him to a Christian college. *Fear.* Worse, I thought I knew exactly how David's life should go. *Pride.*

---

[3] Joyce Meyer, *Battlefield of the Mind: Winning the Battle in Your Mind*, updated ed. (New York: Hachette, 2015).

But surely God wanted David to attend a Christian school, right? This wasn't just about my fear or pride. I was just praying for what he wanted.

God was quiet.

Second, I listened to an old talk by Beth Moore, a well-known Christian speaker. She was recounting how, just after September 11, 2001, she'd been invited to speak at a prayer event in New York, hosted by Pastor Jim Cymbala of The Brooklyn Tabernacle. He hoped she could bring comfort to the terror-torn city.

As Beth sat on a plane headed for New York—one of the first flights allowed back into the city after the attacks—she opened her laptop to prepare her talk. *What could I possibly say to these people?* she wondered. She opened file after file from her archive of past talks, but nothing was appropriate for the world-changing disaster these people had faced.

Feeling completely inadequate, she closed her laptop. "God, I don't have the file for this," she confessed.

She sensed God reply, "Beth, I have the file."

As I listened to her story, I, too, sensed God speak: *Jean, I have David's file.*

In that moment, God's spirit changed me. I felt immense relief in knowing that I didn't hold David's file; God did. I didn't have to force David into my "perfect" plan. God would figure out David's gap year. It wasn't up to me anymore—it never had been.

In the months that followed, David came to me with some "creative" ideas about how to spend his gap year: buying an around-the-world airline ticket (which would take him from place to place in the same general direction over a specified period of time) or moving to South America to become part of a "surfing ministry." *Oh boy.*

I'd listen, trying to keep my facial expression neutral. My heart would react, and I took that as my cue to surrender David's file. *Guide him, Lord.*

WELCOME TO AMSTERDAM

To my surprise, God guided David to the perfect gap-year experience . . . without my help.

"I found this one place," David explained over dinner one evening. "It's a

Christian youth hostel. I'll be a volunteer staff member with different responsibilities each week."

"Sounds great," I said. "Where is it located?"

"Amsterdam."

Oh, Lord. Seriously? Are you kidding? Amsterdam? A month ago, this would have frightened and worried me. But in that moment, I felt complete peace. Clearly something in me had changed. I nodded at my son and smiled.

At O'Hare International Airport with David, John, and Dale as David heads off to Amsterdam.

Despite being located in a city known for decadence, this was indeed the perfect gap year for David. That fall he packed two enormous suitcases, and we drove him to O'Hare's international terminal. As we hugged goodbye, he looked about as happy and excited as a person could be.

Then we heard nothing. For two weeks.

The hostel's dial-up internet service was spotty at best. Finally, we got an email.

"I don't know if God exists," he wrote, "but I think I'll find out while I'm here."

"What?" I said to Dale, showing him the email. "What does he mean, 'I don't know if God exists'?"

I have David's file, God whispered.

And so I prayed. And prayed. Did I mention that I prayed?

The hostel had a small library, and one of David's responsibilities was to take shifts running it. He came across a book called *The Case for Christ*, written by legal journalist Lee Strobel, an atheist-turned-Christian. In the book, Strobel examines the life of Christ with a journalist's investigative eye. This intellectual approach to faith connected with David, and he soon found the answers he was seeking.

When David emailed to update me on all this, I was floored. God had been guiding my son all along. I went straight to the piano and played songs thanking God for everything he was doing in David's life.

We missed David and really wanted to see him in this new environment. Although Dale isn't a fan of international travel, he is a huge fan of his firstborn son, so we flew to Amsterdam in December.

That trip was a major milestone in the way the three of us related. I didn't play Switzerland; instead, over meals, walks, and bike rides, Dale and I listened as David explained everything he was

Visiting David in Amsterdam brought us closer than ever.

learning and experiencing. If David or Dale bristled over something, I didn't intervene. And to my surprise, nothing went nuclear.

"I'm so glad I got over my control issues with David," I told Jill when we got home.

MORE LESSONS IN LETTING GO

Then this email arrived: "I'm not sure I want to go to Cedarville or any small Christian school when I get home," David wrote. "I want to go to Ohio State, and here's why." Then he listed several thought-out reasons.

I dumped my worries onto Jill's kitchen table over coffee. "I don't like this situation," I told her. "What will he be taught at a secular school? And nothing but debauchery goes on in those dorms!"

"You sound frightened, Jean."

"Well, he's only nineteen!" I countered. "Jesus didn't leave home till he was thirty!" I knew I was being a little ridiculous, and we both laughed. But my fear wouldn't relent.

"Remember what you've already learned about letting go," she said. "Maybe you need to apply that to this situation."

I told my dad about my dilemma, confident that he'd be on my side. He listened as I listed all the reasons why choosing a state school would be catastrophic for my son.

"What are David's reasons for wanting to attend Ohio State?" he asked.

I recited the reasons David had listed in his email.

After a long pause, Dad said, "You know, that sounds right to me. He's a different kid than he was a year ago. He made his decision to follow Christ, and it makes sense that he'd want to go there. It just sounds right."

What?

Later that week I called my CAD drafter about some plans I'd sent her.

"How's David doing?" she asked.

People always asked about David. He has one of those charismatic personalities that endears him to people.

I told her that he wanted to attend Ohio State, and before I could launch into all the reasons why this was a terrible plan, she said, "I'm so happy to hear that! I went to a state school, and my roommate was a Christian. That roommate is the reason I know Christ today."

First my dad, and now my CAD drafter. Doesn't anyone think I'm right? Both of these responses gave me pause. *Aren't Christian parents supposed to send their kids to Christian colleges?* Yet two Christians I respected offered me a different perspective. Could it be that I was the one who was off?

During a phone call with David, I was honest about my hesitations. He listened patiently.

"I get it, Mom," he said. "I know it's not what you want, but I'm confident it's the right thing for me. All I'm asking is that you pray about it. Will you do that?"

He had me. Every time David came to mind over the next two weeks, I prayed, *Lord, please convince my son he's wrong.*

It took me two weeks to realize the absurdity of that prayer. Was I telling God what to do? Yes, I was telling the God of the universe what to do. I was bossing God around.

So I altered my prayer: *God, I trust you. Please have your way. Do what you want with David.*

This was better. I was earnestly trying to let go of my desire to control my son.

Then I added a PS: *God, if you really want David to go to a state school, will you let me know clearly—like, through Scripture? Give me a sign.* I wanted to be certain.

Later that week, as I was preparing a Sunday school lesson for the fourth-graders I taught at church, I opened the curriculum and found that the lesson was centered on the life of Daniel—a Bible passage I'd read many times.

The short version of the story is that a teenage nobleman named Daniel loved God and was committed to following him, but when his city was overtaken by the Babylonian army, he was captured and taken to Babylon, a city of secular wisdom with a decadent culture. He lost his family, his church, and his culture. Over the coming years, he was educated by secular scholars and was forced to be part of their secular culture. And yet, through it all, he stayed true to God. In fact, many Babylonians followed God as well because of his example.

The parallels between David and Daniel were too obvious to ignore. I knew God had given me a sign. My son would be heading to Ohio State.

With tears streaming down my face, I closed the curriculum, stood up, and walked straight down the block to Jill's house, where I let myself in the kitchen door. Jill, standing at the sink, took one look at my reddened face and set down the sponge in her hand. "Do we need to go for a walk?"

I nodded.

She put an arm around my shoulder and led me back out the door.

"Jill, I have to tell you what just happened, because if I don't speak it out loud, I'm afraid I will back out of what I sense God wants. I need you to hold me to it."

"You got it," she said. "What happened?"

I told her about Daniel and Babylon, and David and Ohio State.

"I see," she said. "Sounds like God answered your prayers."

"It's so hard, Jill," I said. "But I know it's the right thing."

"Yep," she said. "I think you're right."

I'm sure Jill thought so all along, but she patiently waited for me to arrive there myself.

David went to Ohio State that fall with our blessing, and his faith grew. He made friends. He got involved in a prayer group and a college ministry. It wasn't easy for him, but he thrives in adversity—and of course, God knew this about him all along.

He began college as a business major, but after hearing a talk by a brilliant

God had proved himself more than faithful. He'd earned my trust. I was free from the debilitating need to engineer outcomes.

professor from the Hebrew language department, he changed his major to Hebrew language.

"I want to get closer to the original text of the Old Testament," he explained.

I never would have planned Hebrew language as a major for my son, but by this time, God had proved himself more than faithful. He'd earned my trust. I was free from the debilitating need to engineer outcomes.

David's journey of emancipation into adulthood paved the way for the rest of our kids. I'd learned the hard way that I didn't need to try to micromanage my children's lives.

◊ GOOD LIVING: *Surrender the File*

It's not just teenage children who test our desire for control. I need to ask myself continually, *What person, decision, or situation tempts me to hold on tighter or longer than I should? What would it look like for me to surrender that file to God?*

If you, like me, struggle with trying to control things beyond your grasp, I invite you to reflect on these questions to determine if there's something you need to let go of:

- *What keeps you awake at night with worry?*

- *What person or situation in your life prompts a disproportionate response from you—an excess of anger, anxiety, fear, sadness, etc.?*

- *What relationship in your life needs to enter a new season—one where you carry less responsibility or control?*

- *What is something that makes you think,* That can never happen! Anything but that!

◿ GOOD LIVING: *Find Your Quiet Place*

The best way for me to gain fresh perspective when I feel stuck is to engage in spiritual practices like praying, reading Scripture, and journaling. Sometimes I listen to talks from wise teachers whose spiritual journeys I respect. Sometimes I take a walk or bike ride in nature. I try to find things that help me get out of my head and into my heart. In those spaces, I try to listen for God's discerning guidance in my life. These spiritual pathways quiet my soul and help me stay attuned to God.

- *Prayer:* For me, prayer is just talking to God and doing my best to listen. I'm not listening for an audible voice; I'm listening for thoughts, ideas, and perspectives that I suspect might be God's way of guiding me. If those promptings align with Scripture, God's loving character, and the discerning wisdom of trusted friends, I take them to heart.

- *Reading:* I try to read passages from the Bible each day. I'm surprised how often I discover just the right message for my circumstance. In those moments, I sense God guiding me, saying, *Pay attention, Jean. This applies to you.* I also read authors whose perspectives and wisdom I admire. I listen to audiobooks, podcasts, and sermons—anything to help me broaden my perspective and absorb God's wisdom.

- *Journaling:* For me, journaling is writing a letter to God. I talk to God about whatever I'm facing that day or in that season. It slows my thinking and helps me focus on the issues at hand. I'm not by nature a highly emotional creature, so journaling helps me get in touch with what I'm feeling. It helps me put words to my emotions.

Chapter 9

OVEREXTENDED

Because David had taken a gap year, both he and John were in the same year in college–David at Ohio State and John at Calvin College in Grand Rapids, Michigan. Grace and Dan were busy teenagers at home. The US economy was booming, and my business was growing. I was working with twenty or more clients at a time, and increasingly clients wanted me to design multiple rooms that utilized cabinetry. The pace showed no sign of slowing. It had become more than I could handle by myself.

"With your business doing so well," Dale teased, "I can retire!"

He was getting restless at work. We were way too young to retire, and his comment brought back memories of him suddenly quitting his commodities job when we were newly married. "Please don't quit your job," I said.

But it became increasingly clear that he wasn't joking.

"You know I like my job—I've been there sixteen years, and my boss and customers are good people," he said. "But it's sales, so the travel is never going away. I can see how slammed you are with the business. It's only going to get busier—and you're the chief cook and bottle washer. I'm ready for a change, and if I retire, I could carry some of the load for you here."

"But your job provides our health insurance—and you'd lose your company car," I said.

"Jean, your business is now generating enough income to support us both, even with two kids in college. We can afford to buy our own insurance and get a second car."

I looked at my husband and immediately thought of a dozen important tasks I could offload to him—important things I didn't have time to tackle.

"Could you take over the books?" I asked.

"Absolutely," he said. "If you're willing to surrender them."

I was still doing our accounting by hand—price quotes, purchase orders, invoices, statements, sales tax. I typed everything up and used a calculator to do the math. It was starting to look unprofessional, and it clearly wasn't the way of the future.

I'd always worried about money. Keeping close track of financials gave me a feeling of security and a clear sense of where we were at all times. Handing over that responsibility wouldn't be easy, but it was necessary. Dale was more than trustworthy, so with a mixture of reluctance and relief, I surrendered the books.

And with that, the decision was made. Dale put in his two weeks' notice at work—for the second time in his life—and switched to a new career.

Dale immediately jumped in, transferring our entire business from my ledger to QuickBooks. Over the next five years, he served the business in a million different ways, giving me margin to focus solely on clients and projects. He's the best utility player I could have imagined.

Even with Dale's help, I was incredibly busy. The bulk of my business was designing kitchens for clients who owned beautiful old homes in architecturally rich neighborhoods in and around Chicago. I still conceived and drew all my designs by hand, made all material selections, developed price quotes, ordered all materials, coordinated all deliveries, troubleshot all problems, engineered all the custom cabinetry, and met with clients, contractors, and artisans. It was a lot.

I'd been a business owner now for twenty years, and after decades of word-of-mouth growth, things were really taking off. I hired two young men—sons of family friends—to offload some of the diverse needs of the business. I tried to figure out how to delegate responsibilities to my new employees, but I wasn't very good at it.

Working closely with Dale was new territory too. After so many years of handling the business by myself and being alone while Dale traveled for his job, being together all day, every day required some adjustments.

For one thing, I wasn't used to hearing a booming male voice in the room while I was trying to work. I also got nervous when I overheard his conversations. He and I had very different styles. His assertive tone had been crucial with his industrial sales clients, but this was residential design, and I felt he needed a lighter touch.

"Dale, I think you need to be more patient and a little kinder on the phone," I said. "You're aggressive, and it makes me uncomfortable."

"I disagree," he said. "Vendors need to be pushed, and some clients aren't paying when they're supposed to. You're softer than I am, but I need to be strong in order to tighten the ship."

Oh boy. I didn't like this, but I'd brought Dale into the business to help me, and I agreed with his reasoning. I swallowed hard and let it go.

Since it was upsetting for me to listen to Dale's phone conversations, I moved my office upstairs, out of earshot. If I couldn't hear what was happening, I couldn't get nervous about it. I was prying my fingers off the control lever, one by one.

To my surprise, Dale's approach worked. Clients and vendors didn't get angry the way I'd feared; in fact, they seemed to respect us more when we insisted they deliver as promised. I had been too much of a pushover. It wasn't sustainable to operate like that, and Dale knew it.

The differences between Dale's style and mine were evident in many areas, which led to many challenges and subsequent conversations. But my husband's contributions were invaluable. Jean Stoffer Design was officially a family business.

FAMILY PHOTOGRAPHER

I'd spent years trying to convince myself that my skill with my 35mm camera could produce acceptable portfolio shots, but when I saw the images from my first professional photo shoot, I couldn't believe what a difference a professional photographer could make.

From then on, I carved out a line item in our annual budget to get a few projects professionally photographed. The photographer would shoot images and then scan them with a high-resolution scanner so I could put them on our website.

At the time, our son John, now eighteen and a freshman at Calvin College, was developing a passion for photography. He took classes using my old 35mm camera, and I realized he had a natural eye for framing and lighting.

I wanted to encourage John's talent, but he had outgrown my old camera. The cost of a state-of-the-art digital camera and lens would be significant.

"John," I said one day, "what if the business bought you the kind of camera and lens you would need to take your photography to the next level and, in exchange, you shot my completed kitchens? I'd rather spend our photography money on you than on someone else. The camera would pay for itself quickly, and I love the idea of letting you develop your talent. Plus, it would be fun to have you involved in the business."

It took John about one second to say yes. He immediately started coming up with things he could do professionally if he had a good camera, and he was excited about contributing to Jean Stoffer Design.

"Mom, I think I can make your images as beautiful as your kitchens," he said.

We bought John the camera and lens.

From my habit of poring over foreign design magazines, I'd noticed that the images always looked so much more emotionally evocative than the images in American design magazines at the time. How did photographers accomplish this effect?

After some studying, I finally realized the difference: they only used natural light. The photographers embraced shadows and allowed for a certain mood in each shot. The photography in American magazines, by contrast, was brash.

Every light in the room was turned on, and every nook was flooded with even more light from expensive lighting equipment.

Sunlight is free, and I actually preferred the ethereal feeling in those naturally lit rooms. John and I spent time creating a consistent look and feel for images that portrayed JSD projects.

"Each shot should be so distinctive, so consistently 'Jean Stoffer Design' that people recognize your work as soon as they see a picture," he said.

John experimented with white boards to bounce sunlight around a room. We watched the weather and only photographed on days with some—but not too much—sunlight, which meant we couldn't photograph in January or February in Chicago.

I would stage the shots, then John would figure out camera settings and natural light to shoot them. He was an avid learner, and his skill with the new camera grew quickly. Before long, our photos had a trademark look I loved. Each shot was like a work of art.

Beyond the financial and practical benefits of my arrangement with John, working with a grown child delighted me. It was an excuse to have regular connection, and it felt good to help each other thrive vocationally.

John's ability to capture natural light helped hone the Stoffer look.

During one of our phone calls while John was at Calvin, he told me about real estate in Grand Rapids.

"Houses in my neighborhood near the college are cheap," he said. "Mom, you'd love the old architecture here."

Over the next few years, Dale and I made frequent trips to Grand Rapids to visit John, and I made it a habit to check out the local real estate. John was right—by Chicago standards, there were a lot of inexpensive homes, and the neighborhoods were filled with character.

EDGEWOOD

By 2006, the US economy was doing great, and the real estate market was exploding. It seemed that everyone wanted to remodel their home. Construction dumpsters and remodelers' vans could be spotted on every street.

I was designing plenty of kitchens, baths, laundry rooms, and mudrooms for my clients, but as I surveyed the real estate landscape, I saw a golden opportunity to take on a personal project as an investment. We could purchase an old, tired home with good bones and recreate it as a beautiful, modern home while maintaining all its special architectural details. I got excited about how this would stretch me as a designer—and build our financial portfolio—and I started looking for a "slow-flip" house.

I found such a home on Edgewood Place in River Forest. It was an 1890s Victorian that needed a full-gut remodel but had great potential. We made an offer, and it was accepted.

Having clear boundaries minimized conflict and allowed both of us to move freely and effectively in our own areas of strength.

I'd make all design decisions. Dale would be the general contractor and would select and hire the subcontractors. We would need to replace the home's outdated mechanicals—heating, plumbing, and electrical—and put in all new bathrooms and, of course, a beautiful new kitchen. Then we'd sell the house, hopefully at a nice profit. What could possibly go wrong?

Dale and I were developing a clear division of labor: if it was something that could be seen, it was my decision to make. If it was something no one would see, it was Dale's decision. Pipes and insulation were all Dale. Light fixtures and tile were all me. Having clear boundaries minimized conflict and allowed both of us to move freely and effectively in our own areas of strength.

The sheer scale of the Edgewood project was daunting, and it took a year and a half to complete. We built an addition to create space for a large kitchen, breakfast room, and family room on the first floor, a beautiful master suite on the second floor, and a guest suite on the third floor. We brought in a Bobcat and removed two feet of soil from the basement, which allowed us to finish the basement and create a family room, a walk-in wine cellar, and an exercise room, all with high ceilings.

None of this was cheap. We spent way too much money on this project, and unlike the Lathrop house and the Bvilding, we'd funded much of it with debt. We were in over our heads. If we didn't sell Edgewood quickly, we'd be in financial trouble.

To make matters worse, we'd bought the Edgewood house near the height of an overinflated housing market. As we were completing the home in the fall of 2007, we began hearing whispers about serious problems with mortgage derivatives that could greatly impact real estate values.

I loved the natural light and neutral tones of our completed Edgewood kitchen.

"I can feel something happening in the real estate market," Dale said. "We need to finish this house and sell it—quick!"

As news reports about the fragile real estate climate continued, I was in serious conversations with God about how a crash would affect us. I filled many pages in my prayer journal, explaining to God all the disaster scenarios I foresaw.

Dale and I worked day and night to complete the remodel. Our subcontractors worked their hardest to install cabinet hardware, touch up paint, and hang the last light fixtures. Once everything was in, our kids pitched in with cleaning.

We finished Edgewood in early November 2007, and I was thrilled with how it turned out. I'd designed its spaces with restrained elegance, keeping clean lines on the cabinetry and using more modern light fixtures. The result was a beautiful balance between the house's classic 1890s Victorian architecture and a modern warmth.

It was time to sell. To help get the word out that the house was on the market, we threw a party and invited friends, clients, relatives, and Edgewood neighbors to see the house. We laid out a beautiful charcuterie table, and David and John came home from college for the weekend to serve wine.

I was very aware of the gravity of owing so much money on a piece of property we couldn't sell in the case of a market crash, and I was getting more and more concerned. I prayed every day for a buyer. *God, have mercy. Bring the right person along.*

If the house didn't sell by January 1, I'd need to break the contract I'd signed with Dale about never moving again and put the Lathrop house on the market. We couldn't afford to keep both homes. One of them needed to go!

Winter isn't an easy time to sell a house in Chicago. We held an open house in mid-December, but a huge snowstorm rolled in. Almost no one came.

Right before we were ready to close up, I heard a knock on the door. There on the porch, covered in snow, stood Kim and her husband, Barry—clients of mine. I was currently deep in the design process of their home as they prepared to do a massive remodel. Kim had seen this house in various stages when I'd invited her to stop by and see examples of design features I thought she might want to include in her remodel.

The architecture and design phase of their remodel was nearing completion. They were getting construction bids and making plans to move out for a year while the work was being done. But there were lingering issues with the design, and she realized that given the constraints of their house, it still wouldn't be what they'd hoped for, even remodeled. Could the Edgewood house be the answer to their problems?

I welcomed them inside. They took their time exploring the house, and a few days later, Barry returned, a yellow notepad in hand. Room by room, he took notes. Then we heard nothing.

My money worries were growing by the day as my self-imposed January 1 deadline approached. Would we have to list Lathrop and move?

After Christmas my whole family was in town to celebrate my parents' fiftieth wedding anniversary. We held a big party at our church, and then my siblings and their families headed to our house. By the time we got home, it was after 10 p.m. The phone was ringing when we walked in the door. It was our real estate agent.

"We have an offer," she said.

"Seriously?"

"Seriously," she answered.

"Is it Kim and Barry?"

"Yes," she said, "and the offer is almost full asking price."

Unbelievable.

"Our response is yes," I told our agent. "We accept their offer!"

I was in shock and overjoyed. With my extended family gathered together, I couldn't contain my relief, gratitude, and a hundred other emotions. The celebration continued—with added purpose.

We signed a contract on December 30—just two days before January 1. We wouldn't need to sell Lathrop. *Thank you, God. You knew all along.*

The sale of Edgewood before January 1 was a major marker in my faith journey. I learned to trust God in a deeper way than I'd ever had to before, and as difficult as the in-between time was, I'm grateful for how it stretched me and taught me to depend more fully on God—a lesson I keep learning.

With this offer and its successful closing in February, we felt God had rescued us from financial disaster—especially when the housing bubble did indeed burst a year later. I still shudder—and thank God—every time I think about it.

 GOOD DESIGN: *Involve Your Child in the Business*

John's photography was a natural fit for Jean Stoffer Design, but there are countless other roles a young adult child may play in a company. How might your child be able to contribute to your small business?

- *Space manager:* clean or organize your supply closet, storeroom, or shop

- *Graphic designer:* create ads, logos, and marketing materials

- *Tech support:* create or manage a website; troubleshoot technical problems

- *Social media manager:* create social media posts; write online content

- *Photographer:* take pictures of your products for your website or social-media accounts

- *Event planner:* plan and coordinate details for your business gatherings

◪ GOOD LIVING: *Assess Whether a Family Member Is a Potential Employee*

Inviting an adult child or another family member to be part of your business could be wonderful or terrible. To discern whether a partnership might work, ask yourself these questions:

- *Do they want to be part of the business?*

- *How do they respond to direction from me?*

- *Do I respond to feedback from them?*

- *Do we enjoy each other's company?*

- *Do we share mutual respect?*

If you feel this person might be a good fit, begin with a temporary role. This allows either of you to bow out gracefully with no hard feelings if things don't go well. If you both like the arrangement, then you can increase their involvement.

◪ GOOD LIVING: *Work Well with Your Spouse or Partner*

When a couple works together, differences naturally show up, and that's certainly been true for Dale and me. We lean on these three pillars to keep both our working relationship and our personal relationship solid:

- *Pillar 1: Identify each other's strengths.* Dale's strengths are in diagnosing and fixing the unseen parts of a house—the mechanicals. He knows what needs replacing and how to do it, and he's a remarkably diverse jack-of-all-trades. He's also great at managing subcontractors to execute my designs. My strengths are the big-picture parts of the business—refining our design aesthetic, vision, focus, and specializations. I choose which clients we say yes to, and I do the space planning, interior architecture, and cabinetry design. When we know our own strengths and appreciate each other's strengths, it's easier to assign tasks and then stay in our own lanes.

- *Pillar 2: Show love in conflict.* Dale and I have a handful of recurring conflicts in our relationship. One of them is what it means to be on time.

Without naming names, one of us feels the need to arrive on time, while the other is more comfortable being fashionably late. We've had more lively conversations over this topic than either of us would care to admit, but we both realize that although this issue feels like a big deal in the moment, words said in the heat of the moment last longer and leave a bigger mark on our relationship than whether we're on time to an event. We try to express our feelings calmly, plan ahead for events we attend together, and then resist the urge to get frustrated if things don't go as planned.

- When our kids got engaged, they each watched a series of videos by John Gottman, PhD, a world-renowned psychologist and expert on marital stability. We watched along with them, and we learned that according to Gottman's research, 69 percent of conflicts in a marriage don't get resolved. In other words, the measure of marital success isn't the absence of conflict; it's how you treat each other when conflict arises.[4]

- When Dale and I have conflicts, we strive to talk through them with love and respect. It isn't always easy. Sometimes we need to take a break to collect ourselves before we dive back in. We try to keep the conversation productive rather than focusing on blame.

• *Pillar 3: Take turns.* Over the course of our marriage, Dale and I have taken turns at being the lead breadwinner in our family. We've supported each other's careers. We coparented our kids, which allowed me the space to grow a business. Dale made sure my passion for design had room to develop, and I made sure he didn't languish in a job that sucked the life out of him. Our marriage is a partnership that flourishes best when both parties thrive and we both have room to be who God created us to be. This has required sacrifice from each of us in different seasons. But when we're both working toward the same goal—a marriage and family that supports and loves each other well—the cost of taking turns far outweighs the sacrifice.

---

4 The videos were based on John Gottman, PhD, and Nan Silver, *The Seven Principles for Making Marriage Work: A Practical Guide from the Country's Foremost Relationship Expert* (New York: Harmony, 2015), 137–38.

Chapter 10

BUBBLE EFFECT

We didn't feel the effects of the 2008 housing-market crisis right away, but by 2010 housing values had dramatically decreased. Far fewer homeowners were moving, and most felt it wasn't wise to put more money into their vastly devalued homes. We noticed a dramatic decline in new projects, both with past clients and new ones.

Once the Edgewood house was sold and Dale could spend more time in the office, I made the difficult decision of letting go one of my two employees. Three months later, as business slowed to a trickle, I had to let go of the second one, too.

The timing of the downturn wasn't great for our family. With both David and John in college, Dale and I were making double tuition payments—and Grace would be a freshman in the fall, to be followed by Dan in just three years.

"Our current income from the business won't be enough to sustain us," I said to Dale.

"Between tuition and weddings, we have a lot of expenses coming our way in the near future," he said. "And we've put away almost nothing toward retirement."

We met with a financial planner. After looking over our current financial landscape, he offered some helpful suggestions, but I could tell he was uncomfortable about our future.

It was clear we needed to do something to improve our financial picture before retirement. I remembered what John had said about the affordability of Grand Rapids real estate. Was there an investment opportunity there? I began perusing Grand Rapids homes for sale online.

David graduated from college a semester early, which was a financial relief, and John graduated in May.

"Two down, two to go," I told Dale. But both boys were also engaged, which meant the expenses of two upcoming weddings.

Dave and Kristy's wedding: welcoming a new daughter to our family.

John married Maura that September, and David married Kristy the following February. Dale and I couldn't have been more delighted with our sons' choices. We loved our new daughters as if they were our own—which now they were.

Grace decided to follow in David's footsteps by taking a gap year after graduating high school. She would be volunteering at an orphanage in Bolivia, doing work that fit her personality and passions. We felt great about the organization she would be serving—and a side benefit of this gap year was its timing. Tuition payments for Grace would be postponed a year as we struggled to figure out our new financial paradigm.

With the decrease in new business clients, I was no longer as busy as I had been five years earlier, when Dale came to lighten my load.

"I don't see the economy bouncing back any time soon, so it doesn't make sense for me to keep working for the business," he said one night. "Financially, it would be smarter for me to bring in new income from outside."

We sat there in silence. I knew he was right. But now what? Dale had left his old job–a career in which he'd seen much success–to help me in the business these past five years. If he looked for a new job, what should he do? How does a fifty-four-year-old reenter the job market?

NEW OLD JOB

A week or so later when I got home from work, Dale called me into the living room and pulled me onto his lap.

"I got a phone call today," he said, smiling. "My old boss wants to know if I'd be willing to return."

"Are you kidding?" I asked. "Did he know you're looking?"

"No idea!" he said. "We keep in touch, but I hadn't told him I was looking for work. He just called out of the blue. They really need someone with experience to handle sales in the upper Midwest. These are big accounts, and I already have strong relationships with those customers."

When Dale had left that job, he'd been burned out. We knew that stepping back into the workforce would mean more travel. He would be surrendering the freedom and lifestyle he had come to enjoy.

"What did you tell him?" I asked.

"I told him I'd have to think about it."

"What?"

God knew our needs, and he had provided.

"Just kidding! I told him yes."

No resume writing. No job interviews. The travel would be tough, but he loved the people and knew the role. We both saw this as God's provision at just the right time. It was incredibly good news.

Dale's customers were happy to see him, and there was enough change and newness to make the job feel fresh. He found he really loved his new/old job, and the solid income and benefits helped us survive the downturn in my business.

God knew our needs, and he had provided.

BUSINESS MANAGER

John continued to photograph my kitchens, and he and Maura also shot weddings and family portraits. They hoped to make photography a full-time career, but they didn't have enough business yet to make it financially.

Meanwhile, I needed someone to help me with Jean Stoffer Design. Even though things were slower, I couldn't manage everything on my own without Dale.

I asked John if he would consider working part time as my business manager while he and Maura got their business built up. He jumped at the opportunity, so on Dale's first day back at his job, John started working for me.

As the new business manager, John learned the business inside out. He oversaw billing and scheduled deliveries. He designed a new website that was fresh and easy to navigate, then encouraged me to write blog posts that would make the site more dynamic.

Having John involved in the business proved invaluable. While I brought my years of experience to the table, he offered the insight of a younger generation.

LAKE DISTRICT

David and Kristy had moved to New Jersey so David could attend grad school at Princeton Seminary. The first summer after they got married, they decided to take an extended trip to Europe.

"We'll be renting Airbnbs, couch surfing, and staying with friends from my Amsterdam year," David told me. "Want to join us for the England part of our trip?"

"Absolutely!" I said. "And no doubt it has occurred to you that if I come along, we'll be eating a little better and staying in slightly nicer accommodations."

"Whoa, Mom, those perks never even crossed our minds," he said, grinning. "We just want the pleasure of your charming company."

Inspired by my Cotswold bike trip with Jill, I planned a bike trip for the three of us through England's Lake District. We spent a week cycling through the hilly countryside, coast to coast and then back again. The trip was more strenuous than the Cotswolds because of the terrain—in fact, Kristy gained so much muscle in her legs that it split her pants! But those days were lovely, filled with all the sensory delights I'd enjoyed with Jill. Once again, the sights I saw flooded my idea bank with inspiration.

But the real gift of that trip was spending time with my new daughter-in-law. On some of the harder cycling days, she'd often ride right next to me, talking to me as we worked our way up the hilly terrain.

One day the three of us got caught in a rainstorm and cycled through it until we came across a local pub. Kristy and I made a beeline for the restroom, where we peeled off our wet clothes and tried to dry them with the hand dryer, laughing at the ridiculousness of our situation. That woman is a gem—kind and beautiful and remarkably talented. Day by day together in this incredible environment, we bonded in a way I'll never forget.

It's one thing to get to know someone in your everyday setting, but something magical happens when you enjoy shared experiences outside your comfort zone. Those memories last a lifetime.

It's one thing to get to know someone in your everyday setting, but something magical happens when you enjoy shared experiences outside your comfort zone.

 GOOD DESIGN: *Identify Quality Wood Furniture and Cabinetry*

I'm often asked how to identify quality cabinetry or wood furniture. Here's a rundown of the various elements to inspect when considering a purchase of wood furniture or cabinetry.

Materials

- *Solid wood:* High-end products are made entirely from solid wood that can be sanded and refinished. All the visible parts of our cabinets are made entirely of solid wood.

- *Plywood:* When covered by a thin sheet of solid wood, plywood can be sanded lightly and refinished. Even high-end cabinetry boxes and furniture sides and backs often rely on the strength of plywood rather than solid wood, saving the solid wood for the faces (doors and drawer fronts) and frames. Our cabinets use furniture-grade plywood for the unseen boxes and sides.

- *MDF:* Manufactured wood products made from waferboard or particleboard (sawdust mixed with glue) are often covered in laminate and used for commercial and less-expensive furniture and cabinets. They cannot be sanded or stained. Screws tend to strip easily from engineered wood.

Joints

- *Dovetail:* Solid-wood construction often utilizes dovetail joints, in which drawer faces and sides fit together like puzzle pieces. They're incredibly strong and beautiful. We use dovetail joints for our cabinetry line.

- *Dowels > screws > nails > staples > glue:* Look for these construction methods, listed in order of joint quality and stability.

Finishes

- *Stain plus tung oil or Danish oil:* This finish repels water to some degree but remains porous. It allows fine furniture to breathe but also requires regular reapplication, as it will fade and lose its repellency over time.

- *Nonporous finish:* Furniture or cabinets that receive lots of wear and tear are often finished with polyurethane. This clear finish allows the natural beauty of the wood to shine through while protecting the wood from water damage. It's available in matte or low sheen, making the wood look natural.

- *Painted finish:* Paint can be applied any number of ways, but for cabinetry I prefer a catalyzed painted finish, which is sprayed on and then allowed to cure. A catalyzed finish mixes paint with a hardener right before it's sprayed, yielding a strong, water-resistant finish. Paint that is specifically formulated for furniture and cabinetry can also be applied with a brush.

- *Laminate:* Generally inexpensive and durable, laminate is used for furniture made of particleboard or plywood. It's very water resistant and can't be easily stained or painted. Formica laminate was all the rage in the 1950s–1970s. It still has some pockets of use today, especially for office furniture, countertops, and lesser-quality furniture or cabinets.

Hardware

- *Knobs and drawer pulls:* These are some of my favorite pieces to select, as they have such a visual impact and are touched every day. They come in many finishes, materials, and sizes.

- *Hinges:* On our cabinetry, we prefer hidden hinges that have many points of adjustment and are soft-close. On decorative furniture pieces, hinges can be a design statement. Look for hinges made of solid metal with soft-close technology.

- *Drawer slides:* High-end furniture and cabinetry often use drawer slides that include ball bearings for smooth action, plus hydraulics for a quiet close. I prefer slides that are mounted onto the bottom of the drawer, where they're unseen. Antique furniture sometimes has slides made of wood that wear out over time. Rubbing beeswax or candle wax on the rails can preserve the smooth action and reduce wear.

If buying new cabinets or furniture is beyond your current budget, you can buy used pieces and refinish them. Search Facebook Marketplace, OfferUp, Buy Nothing, local thrift shops, estate sales, or demolition companies to find pieces that fit your needs. With a little sweat equity, you can get quality at a price that fits your budget.

Chapter 11

THE UPROOTING

After finishing her gap year in Bolivia, Grace followed in John's footsteps and attended Calvin College. We loaded her stuff into the back of our SUV for the two-hundred-mile trek from River Forest to Grand Rapids.

"Our car has this route memorized," Dale said. We'd made the drive more times than I could count during John's four years there.

Grand Rapids is a gem of a town filled with culture and economic promise. Located about forty-five minutes east of Lake Michigan, it's a college town with a strong medical community and a robust historical district that dates back to the 1800s. I'd been scanning real estate prices off and on for years, and they were still quite low.

THREE RENTALS

Dale and I were now in our fifties. We'd survived the housing bust of 2008 and now, four years later, the business was once again picking up steam. With Dale's income, we were making ends meet even with the added tuition expense of another child in college. But we still had almost nothing put away for retirement.

After visiting Grace one weekend, Dale and I grabbed lunch in the quaint historical district before heading home to River Forest. "Let's invest in a rental house here," I said. "Grace will be living off campus next year, so instead of us paying rent for her to live in someone else's building, she could live in a house we own—and we could collect rent from her housemates."

"A rental property would also be a fantastic way to build a stream of passive income after she graduates," Dale said. "Let's talk to her and then see what we can find!"

Grace loved the idea. "I have three friends who could move in at the end of May and live there this summer. Then I can join them in the fall!"

In a heartbeat, I was looking online for houses. After becoming frustrated by the lack of updated information on public MLS websites, I found a real-estate agent with real-time information on upcoming listings. We soon came across a three-bedroom house near Calvin that fit the bill. It had just been remodeled by a contractor, which was perfect since May was coming up fast. This place was move-in ready. We took out a small mortgage and paid for the rest in cash.

Three of Grace's friends moved in on the day we closed, and Grace joined them that August for her sophomore year. This saved us money on Grace's room-and-board expenses, and the rent payments from her three friends covered the mortgage and then some—our first step toward securing a stable retirement.

Over the next couple of years, we saved up enough to purchase and remodel two more houses—using cash, not debt. We found two foreclosures that were a mess but were dirt cheap.

"These houses cost less than a new car," Dale said.

"That's because they're filthy and nasty," I reminded him.

"Just our kind of place!"

During the inspections, we made note of everything that needed to be replaced. Then I set to work on the designs.

Over the years I had filled my basement with garage-sale finds, job mistakes, and products left over from previous projects. These quality items were perfect for installing in rentals. We hired a contractor who sanded floors, remodeled the kitchen and bathrooms, painted walls, changed out light fixtures, and cleaned everything up. Our second rental was completed and rented out in just two months.

The repurposed cabinets from my first British-inspired kitchen gave a quality feel to our rental.

It's wonderful when a project goes so smoothly, but I was learning that's not typically the case in a foreclosure. Our third rental property, on Benjamin Avenue, needed more work. The graffiti-adorned house had been a bargain at $36,500. It had good bones, but it was disgusting. Like, hazmat disgusting. I got to work designing it.

I moved the kitchen into the dining room and installed the cabinets from my first English kitchen in the Lathrop house. We'd lived at Lathrop for twenty-plus years now and had remodeled the kitchen again. I'd been saving those used cabinets for a rainy day, and that day was here. We repainted them, and they looked as elegant as ever.

I shopped for quality used appliances on Facebook Marketplace, and we installed brand-new light fixtures I had in storage from mistakes on past client projects. After about nine months, the house was finished and ready to be rented.

Remodeling these rentals was a fun, creative experience in making something beautiful on a shoestring budget. In the end, it was a win for the college students in need of a home away from home and a win for us as newly minted landlords.

MICHIGAN MIGRATION

In the fall of Grace's sophomore year of college, she got engaged to Ted, a young man we liked instantly. Because Grace had taken a gap year before starting college, she was a year older than most sophomores. Still, she was only twenty. Grace had always been wise beyond her years, and this was evident in her choice of a life partner. Ted is as solid as they come.

Grace and Ted married the following summer, when they were both twenty-one and about to start their junior year at Calvin. They moved into the rental house on Benjamin, which we had just finished renovating.

David and Kristy planned to move to Grand Rapids after Princeton, and when Dan finished high school a year later, he chose Calvin as his college. With the exception of John and Maura, who would stay in the Chicago area, it felt as if the center of gravity for our family was shifting to Michigan.

After Dan left for college at the end of summer, our old Lathrop house felt empty.

"Maybe we should downsize," Dale said. "We don't need all this space or the upkeep of a six-bedroom house."

I was ready for this conversation. In fact, I'd been thinking the same thing.

"What's this I'm hearing?" I asked, pretending to be shocked. "I thought you never wanted to move again. Are you saying it's time to revisit the contract you had me sign when we moved here?"

"We should just move to Grand Rapids," Dale said. "We both work from home, so what's stopping us?"

"I'm totally on board with moving near the kids, but it's not as simple for me," I countered. "My entire business is in the Chicago area. All my past clients and projects are here. My business is primarily word of mouth, and in Grand Rapids, I'd be an unknown—and an outsider. I have no idea how to get new business there. I'd be starting over."

"You can keep your Chicago clients and drive back whenever you need to visit a client or a jobsite," he said. "We need boots on the ground to manage the rental properties. It's worth looking at options; that's all I'm saying."

A few weeks later, while driving home from a weekend in Michigan, we approached the Circle Interchange, a chaotic web of intersecting highways in downtown Chicago. I was struck by two feelings: (1) look at how beautiful Chicago is, with its enormous skyscrapers all lit up and Lake Michigan as a backdrop. How could we ever leave this city? And (2) we're crawling along at ten miles an hour on this congested, seven-lane highway. Why do we still live here?

"This is getting ridiculous," Dale said. "Let's move to Grand Rapids."

I began looking for a smaller house in the Grand Rapids real estate listings—not for a rental but for our next home.

I had no idea how (or if) my business would survive a move, but relocating to Grand Rapids felt like the right decision, and I was committed to making one right decision at a time.

FOURTH RENTAL

Dale and I figured it would take six rentals to provide the passive income we needed for our retirement years. We now owned three. Three to go.

David was in his last year of school at Princeton Seminary and was facing a career crossroads. He was no longer feeling a pull toward full-time ministry, which had been his original plan. What would he do next?

"What if we offered David the job of managing the rental properties?" Dale asked. "We could buy a fourth rental, and he could remodel it and live there, rent free. He'd keep the other houses occupied with good renters and help us find more rentals to buy."

I loved this idea. "Kristy is an RN, so she could easily find a job in town," I added. "Let's call them!"

They loved the idea and said yes on the spot. They called back a few weeks later with more good news: they were expecting! *A grandbaby on the way—and a second son involved in the family business! It doesn't get much better than this.*

Soon three of our four kids—and our first grandchild—would be living in Grand Rapids. As a soon-to-be grandma, I upped the urgency of the search for our next home.

Our family expanded to a new generation with the birth of our first grandson, Clark.

David began scouring the Grand Rapids market for another rental so he'd have something to work on as soon as they landed. He found a house with good bones in a good neighborhood, but it was truly disgusting. We seemed to be drawn to the nastiest homes in town.

"'Is it thoroughly disgusting? Call the Stoffers! They'll want it!'" Dale said.

We bought it and David got to work.

ENGLISH COTTAGE

John and Maura welcomed their first child, Frances, in January 2015, and I savored living close to them and my first granddaughter, knowing those moments would be limited once we moved to Grand Rapids.

Nonetheless, I felt a surge of excitement about moving. I'd been happy at Lathrop, and we had lifelong friends in that community. But the idea of moving to a new city—especially one where most of my kids and a new grandbaby lived, and where so many old houses needed remodeling—sounded like an adventure. *Maybe I'm adventurous after all!*

My house hunting continued throughout that spring and summer. I got a FaceTime call from Grace and Ted that fall and learned they were expecting too. It was their senior year, and the baby was due just a few weeks after graduation. This move couldn't happen fast enough.

A granddaughter! Little Frances—compliments of John and Maura.

We came across a midcentury modern home on twenty acres outside Grand Rapids that seemed ideal. We made an offer, but the owners sold to other buyers. We were surprised and a little heartbroken, but the process helped us make the break emotionally from River Forest, the town where I'd lived my entire life, and the house where we'd lived for twenty-five years. Kristy emailed me a Scripture verse, Proverbs 16:9: "We can make our plans, but the LORD determines our steps." I needed to hear that.

When we were in town for Grace and Ted's college graduation in May, I came across a two-bedroom English cottage within walking distance of nearby Reeds Lake in East Grand Rapids. The tiny home had great bones, but boy was it a mess. *Typical Stoffer find!*

I showed it to Dale.

After we walked through each room, he turned to me. "I love the location, but I just can't envision what this house could become," he said. "The rooms are tiny. Even if we updated everything, it would still be a house with a floor plan that would not work for us—or any future buyer. I just don't see it. But if you see it, I can go along with it."

I love that Dale trusts my judgment on such matters. "I think there's enough good stuff here to make something not only workable but truly special," I said. "I need to figure it out, but it's in there somewhere. I know it."

"It's been eight years since the Edgewood project. Have you recovered enough to take on another whole-house project?" Dale asked.

"Yep!" I said. "These rental remodels have primed the pump for me."

"Then let's go for it."

I think there's enough good stuff here to make something not only workable but truly special.

We made an offer on the English cottage on Friday. Ted and Grace graduated on Saturday, and Grace—now thirty-eight weeks pregnant—went into labor and gave birth to a healthy baby, Theo, on Sunday. Seeing my daughter become a mom was a joy like no other. What a weekend!

Tackling our English cottage would stretch my skills. I had designed our entire Lathrop house, but I'd done so one room at a time, over many years. I had designed the entire Edgewood house but sold it unfurnished and unstyled. This project would require not only changing the entire floor plan but also remodeling it and furnishing it fully. It was more comprehensive than anything I'd done before.

I spent the summer and fall traveling between River Forest and Grand Rapids, making plans for our English cottage and packing up the Lathrop house. I started with plans for a moderate remodel, but the impossible floor plan just wouldn't cooperate. As is often the case, "moderate" turned into

Our empty-nest English cottage. Time to remodel!

something much bigger. Still, I restricted myself budgetwise because we were funding the remodel in cash. If my business dried up once we moved to Grand Rapids, we didn't want to be in debt.

David tackled the demo part of the project himself—and promptly discovered a beehive the size of a lampshade inside a closet. But slowly he gutted the house and got it ready for me to begin the redesign.

After giving my eraser a workout, I finally came up with a floor plan. Having complete control over the project simplified everything, because I didn't have to run my designs by a client first. I made sweeping structural changes that greatly improved the house's flow and function. I moved the kitchen to the front of the house, then created a vaulted ceiling by punching into the attic. I increased the size of the living room by moving part of the front exterior wall forward, which created a nook that was perfect for my grand piano.

The two-car garage became the master bedroom, bath, and closets. We added a roomy three-car garage to the back of the house and built a guesthouse above it with two bedrooms, one bathroom, a kitchen, a living space, and a separate entrance. We knew the guesthouse would be a hot commodity. It could be rented out as an Airbnb, and we could control the calendar so the guesthouse would be available for visits from John and Maura or our friends from Chicago.

I got to pick the exact flooring, cabinetry, and finishes I wanted. Whenever Grace and I got together, we'd end up talking about the design. She had a growing interest in everything I was doing, and she had a good eye. It was her first year of teaching school, so we were both taking on new things. I helped her put up bulletin boards in her classroom, and we were glad we had each other.

GOODBYE, CHICAGO

The Lathrop house sold to a new family that fall, with a closing date of December 15. Even though our English cottage was far from being move-in ready, Dale and I decided we'd make the transition to Grand Rapids once Lathrop closed. Grace and Ted were living in our Benjamin Avenue rental, and they invited us to stay with them until the guest house above the garage was finished. Then we'd move there until the rest of the home was complete.

Moving out of a place you've lived for twenty-five years is no small feat, and our new home was much smaller than the Lathrop house, which meant getting rid of about 75 percent of our stuff. We rented a storage unit in Grand Rapids for anything we wanted to keep, setting aside only the essentials to bring to Grace and Ted's house.

As our December moving date approached, the kids wanted to gather one last time in their childhood home, so everyone headed our way for Thanksgiving weekend. We told stories. We reminisced. We laughed. We cooked together, played in the yard, and checked out the remodeling progress of John and Maura's house just a mile away.

At Thanksgiving dinner, we raised our glasses to the ugliest house in town, which had been so good to us over the years. With three grandbabies at the table, a fourth grandbaby on the way (David and Kristy's second), and a new season of life awaiting us in Grand Rapids, we had so much to be grateful for. *Thank you, God. You are so good.*

The next day we rented a huge U-Haul and started loading it. The furniture and boxes were marked either "Storage" or "Benjamin." Our mattress, two counter stools, and two chairs would stay behind until Lathrop closed in a couple of weeks and we would move for good.

"Never again!" Ted, Dave, John, Dale, and Dan after moving my grand piano.

We'd left space at the back of the truck for one final item: the grand piano. I realize there are paid professionals trained in the intricacies of moving a huge, delicate instrument like this. I believe the technical term for these professionals is *piano movers*. But I am cheap. Who needs to hire professionals when YouTube offers free tutorials? I'd done my research, and I had Dale, three grown sons, and a son-in-law to muscle this thing onto the truck. How hard could it be?

I showed the guys the straps and piano board I'd bought on Amazon and then imparted all my YouTube knowledge about how to move a grand piano.

The men went to work. The women stood back and watched, horrified, praying their husbands wouldn't get squashed by a grand piano.

It wasn't going well. We called our neighbors for more help, and soon there were seven men trying to move this behemoth out of the house, down eight steps, up a ramp, and into the moving truck. The guys were covered in sweat, moving slowly and carefully under the weight of this massive piece of wood, wires, and ivory. I wasn't sure what to worry about more: the piano or the people moving it!

When at last the piano was secured inside the truck, the neighbors went home, the wives emerged from their prayers, and my sons looked at me as if to say, *Don't you ever think of asking us to do something like that again!*

Dale turned to me and said, "When we get to Grand Rapids, the guys and I will roll this thing into the storage unit, but after that, we are never touching it again. Ever."

Got it! Not everything that saves money is worth the cost.

A few weeks later, we drove away from our Lathrop house for the last time.

As we pulled onto the freeway, Chicago's skyline rose before us, with Lake Michigan glittering behind it in the frosty morning air. *Goodbye, Chicago. You've been good to us.*

Then we headed east toward Grand Rapids, our new hometown.

⬡ GOOD DESIGN: *Restoration, Renovation, or Remodeling?*

These words often get thrown around as if they mean the same thing, but they don't. If you're considering making changes to your existing home or an investment property, it's helpful to understand what each term entails. Using the right vocabulary will help you communicate clearly with contractors and other professionals.

Restoration

- *What it entails:* the process of returning a house or building to its original condition

- *Cost:* $

- *Best for:* making your building look like it did when it was first built

Restoration is a choice most often associated with historic buildings. Restoration involves projects like removing worn carpeting, refinishing hardwood floors, polishing and repairing window or cabinet hardware, replacing porches or banisters that have deteriorated over the years, and repairing holes in walls, broken fixtures, or broken windowpanes.

Renovation

- *What it entails:* the process of renewing a house by fixing what's already there and possibly adding new elements, while leaving the building's basic footprint intact

- *Cost:* $$

- *Best for:* modernizing a home without changing the current floor plan

Renovation is a choice for any building, whether it's historic, modern, or anything in between. Examples of renovation improvements include replacing cabinetry in an existing kitchen, adding cabinetry to a laundry room, or adding a shower to a bathtub.

Remodeling

- *Definition:* the process of changing an entire room, house, or building
- *Cost:* $$$
- *Best for:* improving the flow, engineering, or openness of a home

Remodeling includes renovation but involves larger structural changes as well. These changes might include removing or relocating walls, stairways, or windows; replacing or installing plumbing, electrical, or HVAC systems; raising the height of existing ceilings; adding bathrooms or living space to increase square footage; or finishing an unfinished attic or basement.

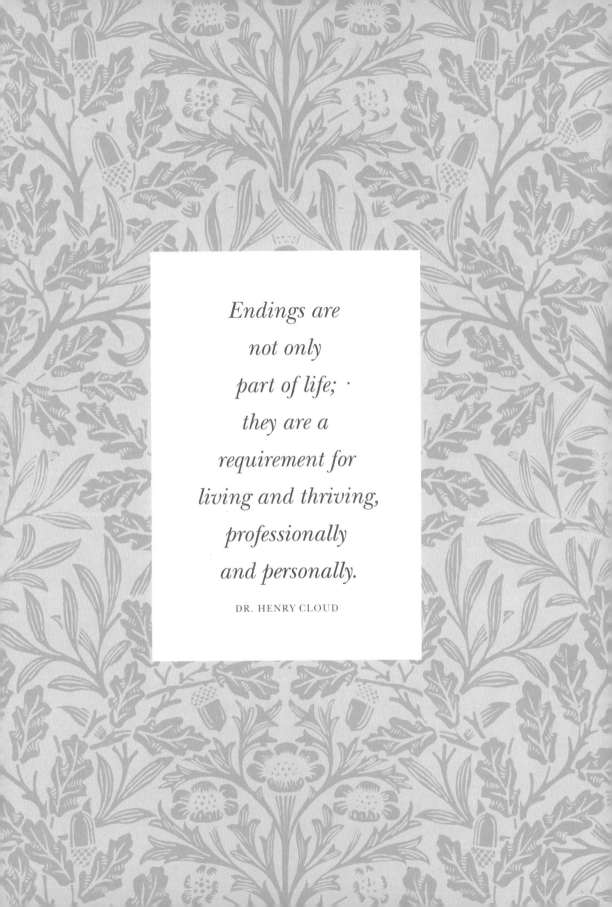

*Endings are
not only
part of life; ·
they are a
requirement for
living and thriving,
professionally
and personally.*

DR. HENRY CLOUD

Chapter 12

HELLO, GRAND RAPIDS

After arriving in Grand Rapids, we got settled in Grace and Ted's home and then hit the ground running. The remodel of our English cottage was in full swing, and our street was a constant mess of construction trucks and dumpsters. I felt a little bad for our new neighbors.

I had noticed that designers in the Grand Rapids area often put signs in the yards of projects they were working on. I mentioned this at a family dinner one night, and David jumped at the idea.

"Your English cottage is on a well-traveled street," he said. "Let's tell people you're designing it."

He commissioned a classy, simple sign, with "Jean Stoffer Design" in large letters. In smaller letters below, it said, "jeanstofferdesign.com." I put it in our front yard, figuring word of mouth had to start somewhere. Maybe this would help.

My first "Jean Stoffer Design" sign at the English cottage.

An early Instagram post, with John's coaching.

INSTAGRAM

Because moving to a new hometown was a risk for the business, I was very interested in raising awareness of our presence in Grand Rapids. I began exploring a new social-media platform called Instagram—and I liked it. I followed my children, and as a proud grandma, I posted photos of my adorable grandbabies. *Who doesn't want to see cute babies—am I right?*

I used Instagram mainly for sharing family photos, but John saw IG differently. In fact, his and Maura's photography business was expanding to commercial work, largely because of Instagram.

When I bought my first iPhone, John and Maura taught me how to take and edit great photos with it. One day, John sat me down.

"All right, Mom. Instagram is becoming a great place for design," he said. "I really think you could generate some interest in your work if you posted shots of your projects. Why don't you start putting JSD out there?"

I started by posting pictures of the progress of our English cottage. When I visited jobsites in Chicago, I would take pictures of those projects and post them, too. While our website with John's gorgeous pro shots was still the primary outlet for showcasing our design work, I enjoyed the personal connection of shooting more casual shots myself, uploading them with captions that just stuck to the facts, like "Kitchen demolition."

John's Instagram captions, on the other hand, were personal. They allowed people to get to know him.

"Don't just give your photos a label," he said. "Write something more informative, like, 'Moved the kitchen into this space with great natural light and opened up the attic to add height. Made such a huge difference!' Now you've piqued people's interest and given them something to comment on."

I took his advice, and over the coming months, I enjoyed experimenting, keeping my captions short and sweet but personal.

FIFTH RENTAL

David found a new rental for us to buy—a four-bedroom home on Martin Street. It needed everything. I know—shocking.

"Great news!" David joked. "I found a small spot in the back bedroom closet that doesn't need remodeling!"

David served as the general contractor for the entire project. By this time, David and Kristy's son Clark was a toddler, Kristy was working full time as an RN, and they'd welcomed baby Charles to their family. When Kristy went back to work following her maternity leave, David took charge of caring for their two kids. Mixing those responsibilities with remodeling was a scramble. Since he couldn't do much of the hands-on work himself, he hired subcontractors and managed the crews, ordered materials, and kept everything on track.

ENGLISH COTTAGE REDUX

Our English cottage moved along at a good pace. By June, the guest house above the garage was complete, and Dale and I moved in. All that remained was the finishing work of the main house—and I really wanted craftsman-level quality there. I hired a tile setter, wood-floor installer, trim carpenter, and painter. David and Dale hung all the light fixtures and installed all the hardware.

When I posted shots of the progress on Instagram, people seemed really interested. They wrote insightful comments, which inspired me to post more pics.

By August, the project was complete. It had taken a little over a year to utterly transform this home with its challenging floor plan. We had increased the home's footprint from 1,700 square feet to 2,900 square feet, and from

My piano found a home in the living room of the English cottage.

Sometimes saving a few bucks just isn't worth the cost.

---

two bedrooms/one bath to five bedrooms/three baths, including the guest house above the garage.

I chose every finish to work together as a whole. With my British-inspired cabinetry designs in the kitchen, laundry room, and baths, and with the variety of materials and textures we'd chosen, the house was warm and classic, but with a modern twist.

On move-in day, the first piece of furniture to make its way into the house was my grand piano, which had been in storage since Thanksgiving. I hired two professionals, and it took them all of five minutes to move the piano from storage into their truck, then another five minutes to unload it into my living room. I was flabbergasted, recalling how I had almost killed my husband, sons, and two neighbors trying to save a few bucks by loading that beast ourselves. Lesson learned.

Once the rest of our furniture and boxes were unloaded, I took my time unpacking and setting everything in place. It was the first time I'd ever moved into a home I'd fully remodeled, and boy, did I love it! Every corner of the house had been conceived, drawn, and coached through to execution. It was gratifying to be the person who got to enjoy it. I hung the paintings my grandpa had given me years ago, and we settled into our empty-nest, grow-old-together house.

BLOCK PARTY

We'd been in town for several months, but Jean Stoffer Design was still unknown in Grand Rapids. Most of my business was still coming from past clients and word of mouth in Chicago. I wanted to break into my new town's market as a designer, but I wasn't sure how.

Then we got a knock on our door from a neighbor we'd met during the remodel.

"Hey, we haven't had a block party in ages, and you're our first new neighbors in years," he said. "It would be great to reconnect and give you a chance to meet everyone."

"Sounds fun!" I said. "How can I help?"

"Well . . . true confession: we're all very curious about your project. So what do you say we have the block party on your driveway, and maybe neighbors could get tours of the house? If you're willing, that is."

"Considering all the construction traffic and mess you guys have put up with during this remodel, I say it's the least we can do!"

Dale and I loved the idea of meeting our new neighbors in a friendly, laid-back atmosphere—and I loved the idea of opening our home.

At the block party, I gave tours and answered lots of questions. Evidently my design style wasn't typical for West Michigan, and I was pleasantly surprised by how positively people were responding to it.

Grace and Ted had come to the party, and after everyone else had left, my daughter drew up a stool at the kitchen island and pulled me aside.

"Mom, your neighbors loved the house," she said. "And I really loved being your sounding board on all your

The completed English cottage: airy and light, with plenty of room for family!

selections here. I know you only design kitchens and baths, but if you ever get a request for designing a whole house, furniture and all, do me a favor and don't say no right away. Call me! Maybe we could do it together."

Grace picks things up quickly, and her interest in design had grown exponentially since she'd been helping me with the house. She and Ted had purchased a duplex, and she was enjoying experimenting with design on a shoestring budget.

"I would only consider saying yes to a full-house project if you did it with me," I said. In addition to having a good eye, Grace was a hard worker, and I loved spending time with her. "We could figure it out as we went, and I could draw on my experience from before you were born."

The two bedrooms at the English Cottage.

The more I thought about it, the more doable it sounded. My whole-house English cottage project had come together beautifully with Grace's input. Maybe we could offer this same experience to others.

We'd arrived in Grand Rapids at an ideal time. Older neighborhoods were filled with vintage homes that had great bones but were in need of a designer who would respect their past while helping them reach their full modern potential. My passion for remodeling old homes wouldn't be wasted here, if only someone would give this unknown designer a chance.

The timing for Grace seemed doable too. She taught preschool part time, but she wasn't thrilled with her job. I reminded myself that it was just an idea for now. We'd have to wait and see.

An adorable young couple, Jenna and Ben, and their two small children were among the block-party guests that night. Jenna loved everything about our house. She loved the reclaimed barnwood floors and beams; she loved the windows; and most of all, she loved the kitchen. She pulled Ben in to take a look.

"See! This is it exactly!" she told him. To me she added, "We just bought the house up the street on Lakeside, and we're going to do a large-scale remodel of the whole house, but the design phase isn't going well. I've been trying to describe the look I'm going for to potential designers, and your home is it exactly—especially the kitchen! This captures what we want. It's perfect."

Ben totally agreed. Inside, I was jumping up and down, hoping they might become my first Grand Rapids clients.

I woke up the next morning to an email from Jenna in my inbox.

"Ben and I talked when we got home last night, and we both felt immediately you would understand what we're trying to accomplish with our house," she said. "I know you're a kitchen designer, but obviously you know how to design all areas of a home. Plus, you've raised four kids, so you understand the needs of a growing family. Could we talk to you about doing all the design work for our project? When might be a good time?"

"Okay, this is exciting!" I showed Dale the email.

I called Grace. "Were you serious about working with me if I got a request for full-service design?" I told her about my brief conversation with Ben and Jenna the night before. "They just emailed. They want to hire me for their whole house."

Grace's response: "I'm all in."

She cut back her teaching job to two mornings per week, and we said yes to partnering on a full-service design for Jenna and Ben.

SIXTH RENTAL

Dale had been back at his job for seven years now, with a total of twenty-two years with the company. He was once again getting tired of the travel and was ready to enter a new phase of life. As the year came to a close, he retired and took over the remodel on the fifth rental house, freeing David to attend to other business ventures and family commitments.

We bought our sixth and final rental property soon after, and it was in the filthiest condition of anything we'd ever purchased. It took a year to complete, with Dale doing much of the work himself and hiring out the rest. But Dale and I had worked on countless remodel projects together in our thirty-six years of marriage, and we were a well-oiled machine: I planned the design and Dale executed it.

When the last bit of work was done and a new family moved in, we felt a sense of relief—not only because we now had six rentals to augment our retirement years, but because those rentals provided six families with a beautiful place to call home.

GOOD BUSINESS: *Build Your Social Media Following*

Social media can give you a whole new way to connect with people and increase awareness of your business. Here are some tips I've adopted along the way that you might find helpful:

- Keep your professional social-media accounts separate from your personal ones.

- Personalize your captions on photos to help readers get to know you.

- Develop a brand of photography that reflects your style.

- Only post photos that represent your brand. Posting subpar photos breaks trust with your followers.

- Whenever possible, respond to reader comments. Nothing boosts viewership like seeing responses from the owner of the account.

GOOD DESIGN: *Remodel a Rental Property*

If you are considering purchasing a rental property, it's important to recoup your investment. Here are three principles we use to guide our remodeling decisions for rentals:

- *Choose neutral colors.* When you're selecting paint, cabinets, and flooring, make sure the choices will appeal to a variety of tenants. This allows renters to personalize the home with their own furnishings and wall decor. It's more cost effective to buy one color of paint in a five-gallon bucket than to buy different colors in one-gallon cans. Sticking with one color also simplifies touch-ups.

- *Choose durable flooring and countertops.* These features get lots of wear and tear, so invest in higher quality and greater durability. Less expensive options might save you money in the short term but will cost more in the long run when they need replacing. In addition, quality flooring and countertops help draw higher rental income.

- *Look for high-quality used items.* Search Facebook Marketplace or OfferUp for used pedestal sinks, light fixtures, or even appliances. When inspecting sinks, check for cracks or chips. Make sure light fixtures and appliances work! When choosing an appliance, look for something that is relatively new and research its repair history online using the manufacturer's name and the unit's model number.

Chapter 13

TIPPING POINT

I was especially happy with how the kitchen turned out in our new home. The success of our English cottage gave me the confidence to say yes to whole-house projects in general, and best of all, it had drawn my daughter into the business.

I had no doubt I would love working with Grace. When we started on Jenna and Ben's Lakeside house that fall, she often brought along baby Theo, which brought back memories of my early days in the business, when I'd been the young mom and Grace had been the baby. The sweetness of our new arrangement was not lost on me.

I loved whole-house design, but my passion for kitchens hadn't changed. If anything, it grew stronger. I truly believe the kitchen is the heart of every home.

I truly believe the kitchen is the heart of every home.

Going forward, Jean Stoffer Design would be a kitchen-centric, full-service design firm. It had taken almost thirty years of experience to get to this point—three decades of learning to draw the most intricate cabinetry details and becoming proficient at space planning, appliance integration, client service, vendor relationships, financial management, contractor communication, and marketing. I'd learned to celebrate successes and fix my mistakes, and I was excited to see where this new turn would take us.

INVERWAY

A week after signing on to design Jenna and Ben's house on Lakeside, I received an email from Josie, a kitchen client from the northwest suburbs of Chicago. Josie and her fiancé, Chris, were getting married in a few months, and their blended family would include five teens.

The house on Inverway had once been a one-room schoolhouse. They clearly needed more space and were in the design phase of a massive gut/remodel/addition.

"We love your design plans for the kitchen," Josie said. "In fact, Chris and I love them so much, we're wondering if you would help us design the whole house. This is our first place together, and we need help blending our styles. We want all the selections to be cohesive and handsome, but they also need to work for our family. It's overwhelming. Please consider helping us!"

I loved Josie and was interested in helping her on this project. I called Grace and described what needed to be done. Everything would need to be laid out and selected, and we'd be starting from scratch. "Want to take on a second whole-home project? This one is in Chicago."

She was thrilled. "Let's do it!"

We met with Chris and Josie so I could hear their vision for their new home. Grace and I took copious notes on everything from room flow to style preferences.

I sent them a contract that detailed the scope of services for the entire house—cabinetry layouts and designs, plumbing fixtures, light fixtures, countertops, tile, furniture, rugs, wall treatments, window treatments—everything down to the last throw pillow. They signed.

The past fourteen days had been a whirlwind. I'd given tours of my first whole-home project (our own house) in our brand-new hometown, I had added a business partner (my daughter), and I'd said yes to two new whole-house clients—on top of my usual number of kitchen and bath clients. It was a lot, but I was excited by the challenge.

LAKESIDE

At the Lakeside house, our client Ben hired his brother-in-law, Cory, to be the general contractor. Grace and I would work with Jenna and Ben to create the design, then Cory and his team would execute it.

Working with Cory made for a great partnership. He was about the same age as David and already had significant experience in construction management. He was the third generation of a family home-building business that offered new-home construction, but he was interested in remodeling older homes.

I was impressed with the way Cory organized the jobsite and managed his subcontractors. He was always prepared with whatever a subcontractor would need—spec sheets, installation drawings, product information, and materials. The jobsite was always clean, and the atmosphere was one of cooperation, with everyone doing their best to help each other out. I had never experienced anything like it.

Within a few weeks of working with Grace on the Lakeside and Inverway designs, I could tell she was the perfect partner—even after she sprung some fun news.

"How flexible can you be with my schedule?" she asked. "Because you're going to be a grandma again in the spring!"

"Well, that's exciting!" I said. "Every time I turn around, one of you is announcing that a new baby is coming." Grace's baby would make grandchild number six—all under three. "I need another Pack 'n Play!"

"I'm due in April," she said. "When I go on maternity leave from my teaching job, I really don't want to go back. I'm yours permanently, if you'll have me."

"That makes me very happy," I said. "You know from your own childhood what this schedule is like for a mom. There will be some travel to Chicago, but you can take the baby along. Most of our work can be from home, and I'd be willing to accommodate your situation."

"Awesome," she said.

We both would be doing what we loved and staying closely in tune with our families.

It's a joy to take work trips with Grace. Here we are in Chicago.

Three of our four kids were now enhancing our lives with their professional skills: David as property manager of our rentals, John as the chief photographer (and unofficial social-media coach), and now Grace as my design partner. They each added so much, and our relationships grew deeper and stronger as a result. Family dinners became energetic brainstorming sessions as we continued the steep learning curve of growing a business.

Grace and I worked together in a way that took advantage of each of our strengths. My job was to space-plan everything, design the kitchen and bath layouts and cabinetry, determine furniture layouts and lighting plans, and make sure everything was scaled properly. Grace selected all the finishes, fabrics, lighting fixtures, hardware, and tile. She worked with me two days a week, and on the other three days I worked on my kitchen-only projects and handled the business end of things.

Grace and I worked together quickly and efficiently. We constantly ran our ideas past each other for review and input, and we were usually on the same page.

A lot had changed since my days as an interior designer in the 1980s. Most vendors could now be found online, which made sourcing materials much simpler. However, I had been out of the business of buying furnishings for a long time, and Grace was brand-new, so we had a lot to learn.

Choosing the right furnishing pieces for a remodel happens early in the process, as most clients can't envision how a room might look without knowing what furniture will be in it. By the time a house remodel is complete, almost everything has already been ordered and is either in transit or is sitting in a local warehouse awaiting delivery.

As soon as Grace and I began looking for Lakeside's furniture and decor, we faced a real challenge.

"Where do other designers shop for this sort of stuff?" Grace asked.

"When I designed in Chicago, I sourced products at the Merchandise Mart. But that was before the internet, and we're not in Chicago. So I think we need to start looking online. I've been seeing a buzz on Instagram about the High Point Market."

High Point Market is a massive trade show held in North Carolina twice a year. It covers entire city blocks—millions of square feet. Thousands of manufacturers set up showrooms there to display their offerings.

"We should go this spring!" I said.

We looked up the dates for the next High Point Market, and it was scheduled for the week of Grace's due date. That wasn't going to work. Instead, we ordered several pieces of furniture for Lakeside from retail sites and a few from trade-sourced sites, which had pieces that were more distinctive.

Dale agreed to go with me to High Point that spring. When we arrived, I had no idea what to do, where to go, or how to navigate any of it. Thankfully, a designer I followed on Instagram was attending High Point too, and she sent me lists of all the exhibitors I should check out and places to eat, along with tons of insider information.

Dale and I spent three days at High Point, and I connected with the reps of some furniture companies that would be good sources for our full-service interior design projects. They promised to follow up with a visit to help us learn their lines more fully.

That fall, once the remodeling of Ben and Jenna's house was finished, Grace and I hit the stores to find pillows, art, plants, and decor that would make the house feel like a home. We were developing a distinct aesthetic and were looking for decor that fit into it.

In a few short days, we cleared out Target, HomeGoods, and the local nursery, purchasing everything we thought might work nicely with the items we'd spent months selecting online.

The cool blues and warm brass and wood create a stunning contrast in the Lakeside project.

Start to finish, Ben and Jenna's Lakeside design and remodel took twelve months to complete—and it was gorgeous. Cory's crew had implemented our design with care, and Grace and I felt proud of the way the furniture and decor had come together. Best of all, Jenna and Ben loved everything, which was our ultimate sign of success.

TIPPING POINT

In the fall of 2017, John posted a picture of our English cottage kitchen to his Instagram account. He had been an early adopter of IG and now had a significant following. His post got a positive response, and several leading inspiration accounts reposted it, crediting him with the photography and me with the design. I then posted the same picture on my account so when people saw an image of my work elsewhere, they would see more images of the same space—and maybe choose to follow me.

Over the next few weeks, my IG following grew from a few hundred to more than a thousand. I posted a few photos from the Lakeside house, along with some cute grandbaby pictures, and people responded to the Lakeside photos in droves.

Then John called.

Young people know stuff, and it pays to listen.

"Okay, Mom, you now have about five thousand followers, and they are there for design," he said. "You need to stop posting photos of your grandkids on your Instagram feed. I know you're a proud grandma, but this is your professional account. Your followers are here to see your design work. Deliver what they want. No more babies in bathtubs. Every photo you post must be really good. Don't just throw any old photo up there. Then let's see what happens."

From then on, I posted only excellent shots of my design work, just as John had coached me. More people began to follow.

A few days later, John called again. "Hey Mom," he said, "Maura and I were talking, and she thinks you need to change your IG handle to @JeanStofferDesign instead of just your name. It needs to be clear that you're a professional designer—and that this is your business account."

Right again. Young people know stuff, and it pays to listen. I made the change as soon as we hung up.

John and I had worked hard over the years to develop our Jean Stoffer Design photography aesthetic. Each photo was like a small work of art. Per John's coaching, I only posted photos that met this standard, and our designs were starting to get recognized.

For a designer trying to gain traction in a new hometown, Instagram was a huge win. Prior to Instagram, the only way to get exposure for completed projects was to put them on our website and hope someone stumbled across the site or to get them published in a magazine, where a few people hold the keys and the lag time is often a year or two. Getting published in a book or magazine is like winning an Oscar.

Instagram, on the other hand, is like winning a People's Choice Award. Anyone can vote. If people like what they see, that account gains traction. And the response time is hours instead of years.

I really enjoyed the real-time feedback of Instagram. People wrote interesting comments on my posts, and if they had questions, I did my best to respond.

In October of that year, my Instagram account got a substantial boost when @ChrisLovesJulia reposted a picture I'd taken of a little nook in Ben and Jenna's bedroom. Chris and Julia Marcum are a wildly popular husband-and-wife DIY team, and they have a loyal following on Instagram. When they posted this photo, Jean Stoffer Design was instantly introduced to hundreds of thousands of followers. In less than twenty-four hours, I went from having a little more than 5,000 followers to 10,000 followers—and growing.

We'd reached a tipping point.

When Josie and Chris's home on Inverway was ready to be styled, Grace and I again hit Target and HomeGoods, only to find the exact same items we'd seen when shopping for the Lakeside house.

"Uh-oh," Grace said. "We can't style these two projects the same way!"

"Absolutely not," I agreed. "Back to the drawing board."

We started searching for items from online suppliers but found it difficult because they rarely showed what items looked like in an actual room.

"This isn't sustainable," Grace said. "What will we do for our next project?"

"I don't know," I said. "We have to find a way to style an entire home in

The completed Inverway project creates a welcoming space for the owners' large family.

short order, with unique, quality items. Here in Grand Rapids—in fact, in most cities—that just isn't an option."

"We should open our own store. That would solve it!" We both laughed.

We furnished Chris and Josie's home with beautiful pieces I found while at High Point and styled the home with an assortment of pillows, art, and objects gathered from a myriad of stores, antique shops, and nurseries.

When we walked Josie and Chris through their completed home, the look on their faces said it all.

"This is us exactly!" Josie said. "How did you manage to deliver a design that makes us feel so at home?"

"I took cues from how you dress," I said. "Your style is . . . sophisticated with a flair."

"Well, it worked, because that's exactly how this house feels. I absolutely love everything about it. You helped us find our style."

Grace and I now had two full-service design houses under our belts—three, counting our English cottage. When I'd completed a kitchen project in the past, I'd often feel a little dissonance. I'd be more than pleased with the kitchen itself, but since I wasn't yet offering full-service design, the adjoining rooms often didn't match the heightened aesthetic of the kitchen.

Our whole-house projects, by contrast, were comprehensive. Every corner of the house was designed. The furniture, lighting, wall treatments, and decor went together perfectly. It was a joy to see these projects completely designed, down to the last detail. The completed homes were deeply satisfying.

◊ GOOD LIVING: *Empower Your Adult Child or Family Member in Your Business*

Grace was a perfect fit as a designer and consultant for my business, but we test-drove working together before Grace quit her job to come on board. Working with my adult children in the business is a great joy, and I've learned a few things along the way:

- *Divide and conquer.* Rather than trying to share the same parts of your business with your adult child, find an area of responsibility where they are naturally more gifted than you and let them grow that part of the business. This keeps the running lanes clear.

- *Delegate.* This means surrendering parts of the business to others and letting them become the expert in that area. If your business partner is your adult child, this will mean a role reversal. Keep in mind that your family member will make different (sometimes better!) choices than you. Loosen your grip— it's part of the growing process.

- *Affirm each other frequently.* Every person you lead—including family members—appreciates your approval. Be generous with your words of affirmation when they do things right. Acknowledging their skill and ability strengthens your working relationship.

- *Give honest feedback.* No matter how skilled your family member may be, they'll still need your input and guidance at times. Coach them with respect while allowing them to experience the natural consequences of their mistakes. Being the child of the boss can make a young adult the bull's-eye of disgruntled or jealous employees. Take off your rose-colored glasses so you can see your child accurately, or if you're prone to being overly critical, go out of your way to affirm your child, both privately and publicly.

- *Own the failures.* If your child or family member makes a mistake or something doesn't go well, take responsibility for it with your client, rather than casting blame and pointing a finger. As the overseeing adult, whatever went wrong is ultimately your responsibility. Don't blame or shame your child; rather, coach them privately and work together to learn from mistakes. Ask for their feedback as well. Being open to constructive criticism adds value to your relationship.

- *Remember who's boss.* If you hesitate to cross your family member for fear of wounding them, be brave. Ultimately, your business is something you grew and are now inviting them into. Don't be shy about making big decisions and letting your voice be heard. As long as their voice is also heard, the work environment can strike a healthy balance.

- *Give away the glory.* When things go well, don't steal the glory. Give credit where credit is due. This increases job satisfaction and improves the work culture.

- *Make new memories together.* We take a Stoffer family vacation for one week every summer. We rent a home within driving distance and spend the week cooking, eating, talking, playing, and just being together. No one ever misses out on gathering for those seven days together, and it strengthens our family bond.

Chapter 14

MEETING THE MADISON

After Lakeside was finished, Cory hosted a party there to celebrate. He and I were like proud parents, telling stories about the remodel and answering questions while friends, family members, and clients toured the house.

"We need to do another project soon," Cory told me. "We work really well together."

I liked the sound of that idea.

At the party, a current kitchen client of mine, Joel, approached me with a smile.

"I found your next project, Jean," he said.

"Oh, yeah?" I asked, intrigued.

"Yes. It's a massive old home in the Heritage Hill neighborhood. It's been on the market for a couple of years, and the price keeps dropping. All the original architectural goodies are still there. It's in rough shape, but it could be beautiful."

I shook my head. "Joel, you know I love old houses, but Heritage Hill? In the historic district? It's probably a protected historic structure, which means too many rules to follow and too many committees to get permission from. No thanks. Too complicated and too expensive."

In a historic district, every change to the exterior of a house needs to be pre-approved by a historic preservation committee, and I'm not a fan of committees.

Joel didn't give up. He called a few weeks later.

"Your next project just dropped by $100,000," he said. "Jean, you should at least look at the place."

My curiosity got the better of me, which was how Dale and I found ourselves on Madison Avenue in the Heritage Hill historic district of Grand Rapids, just three miles from our English cottage. A Greek revival estate home on a hill stood before us.

In the twenty-four hours since Joel's call, I'd done my research on this house. I had learned that several interested parties had considered buying it, but none followed through because their plans were contingent on getting the zoning changed from residential to commercial. Every buyer wanted to turn the house into a wedding venue, an event space, or a boutique hotel. But the city and the historic preservation committee weren't having it. No one was interested in keeping the house as a single-family home. It was a large house that appeared to need literally everything to bring it up to working order.

When I pulled up the listing online, I realized how huge the house really was—a whopping ten thousand square feet of former glory on four floors.

I'd pored over dozens of photos and videos, exploring each room and memorizing the floor plan as I clicked. The more I explored, the more intrigued I became.

The home was built in 1902. A formal staircase swept from the front hall to the second floor. A second staircase—narrow, winding, and built for the home's servants—started in the basement and snaked all the way up, providing the only access to the attic. The first floor had ten-foot ceilings. The second floor's ceilings were a respectable nine feet, and even the attic ceilings were lofty and open.

The roomy basement included a ballroom, a garage, and the home's outdated engineering systems. All told, there were four floors, seven bedrooms, seven baths, five distinctive fireplaces, and several living spaces, including two huge sunrooms. Apparently, it had been a boardinghouse at one point. *Hmm. That sounds familiar.*

I'm a total sucker for a deal, and with the price drop, this one-of-a-kind property was inching toward the "good deal" category. The purchase price included a total of five lots in the heart of the Grand Rapids historic district, with the house itself occupying only two of those lots. The other three consisted of usable, buildable land in the resurgent historic district, where land was scarce. Those extra lots held potential of their own.

The Madison's original formal staircase blocked guests from the heart of the home—the kitchen.

But for me, the most appealing part of the property was the sunroom at the back of the house.

BIG, BAD, AND BEAUTIFUL

"I really want to go see it," I told Dale at dinner.

"I am totally uninterested in a project of that scale," he replied. "It would be a repeat of Edgewood. I just retired, and I don't want the risk of adding something of this magnitude to our lives."

"I get it," I said. "I just want to take a look."

"No commitment?"

"No commitment."

"Fine," he said.

My husband is a saint.

As we waited for our real estate agent, Dustin, to arrive, we walked up the crumbling brick driveway that circled a sprawling, overgrown backyard.

"The house is wider from this angle than from the front," Dale said.

"Oh my gosh, just look at those sunrooms," I said.

Dale was right. Twin enclosed porches attached to the back of the house, extending out to the sides like a T. This added a good fifteen feet of width to each side of the main house and easily twenty feet of depth.

Between the sunrooms lay a concrete terrace leading to a back entrance. We climbed its cracked stairs and looked around, taking note of what the photos had failed to reveal about the house's exterior.

Paint peeled from every window sash—of which there were many—and the brick walls had clearly gone decades without tuck-pointing or a good

The Madison's twin sunrooms and back terrace were a mess, but they screamed potential.

power wash. The terrace was in terrible condition, with cracks in the concrete that showed heavy water damage and several generations of feebly attempted repairs. No doubt rain and melting snow had been leaking into the space below for decades. Some sort of vinyl roofing material was laid haphazardly across the cracks.

When Dale placed a hand on the terrace railing, it almost fell off. "It's totally rotten," he said. "The terrace isn't properly pitched to allow rainwater to run off. Water just sits here, eroding the concrete and any wood it touches."

Oh boy. The house had been vacant and neglected for years, and it showed.

"I'm guessing every system in the house would need to be replaced—heating, plumbing, electrical," Dale said.

"I'm sure you're right," I said. "The exterior is in rough shape, but it's gorgeous, too. Maybe the same is true inside."

I stepped toward the sunroom on our left, wiped spiderwebs from a dust-caked windowpane with my shirtsleeve, and peered inside. My heart skipped a beat.

"Oh, Dale. Come look!" I whispered.

The listing photos hadn't done justice to the sunroom. It was huge and bare, and even dust and neglect couldn't mask its sheer beauty. An imposing fireplace stood against the interior brick wall. The other three walls featured French windows—thirteen sets in all—with glass transoms above and wood paneling below. Morning light cast a warm glow across the rough concrete floor.

Already I could picture how incredible this space could be: a sunny, four-season room with glass walls and transom windows that would give families the sense of being outdoors enjoying fresh air, even during inclement weather. The vintage radiators that lined three walls and the brick fireplace at the back would give even the coldest of Michigan winters a run for its money.

"Dustin's here," Dale said. A car pulled into the brick driveway behind me. Dustin was the son of good friends of ours and a successful real estate agent. He had found two of our rentals (both of which were disgusting, so he knew we'd love them).

"Hey, guys!" he said, making his way up the terrace steps.

We chatted for a bit, then he pulled out some paperwork. "I talked to the city about the vacant lots next door and confirmed they're part of the property bundle," he said. "They're definitely buildable, which could figure nicely into any investment decision. Take your time and look around."

He unlocked the back door and held it open. "Let me know if you have questions," he added. "I may have the answer, but if not, I'll look into it."

Dale and I wandered each room, checking everything out. The house was completely bare, which allowed us to examine it without furniture to distract us. The condition of the interior was as bad as we'd feared. When we turned on faucets, brown water spurted out. Windows were painted shut. Every wall in the entire house was covered in outdated wallpaper. *What's it covering up?* I wondered.

Every room smelled musty and damp. The ivy growing on the outside of the house had found its way through many of the windows and was now creeping across the floor and climbing up interior walls.

"Look—an indoor garden!" I joked.

The basement was a mess. A massive boiler sat rusting in the corner. Hundreds of wires and pipes—some in use and some abandoned—hung from the ceiling.

Dale, my resident expert on all things unseen, inspected the mechanical systems of the house.

When a home has good bones and quality craftsmanship, even dust and neglect can't mask its beauty.

"It has all the original wiring, plumbing, and heating," he said. "There's really nothing good here. The heating system looks functional, but there is no air-conditioning—and no air ducts in the walls."

Now I know why this house is still sitting here, I thought. *It's big and bad . . . but also beautiful.*

Decades ago, a fire in the attic had necessitated a remodel to that area. Modern foam insulation covered the roof rafters.

"Well, it has that going for it!" I said.

"It's the only insulation in the entire house," Dale said. "Not good for a house in Michigan."

Every room in the house was dated but full of character.

Except for the condition of just about everything, the house was magnificent. The craftsmanship was stunning, and every room brimmed with character. The original hardware was intact—glass knobs, brass handles, brass door hinges, and ornate radiators. Detailed woodwork and divided-light windows were all original, albeit chipped and rotten in many places. The solid mahogany doors were in great shape.

Then I noticed the floors. *Rift and quartersawn white oak!* This type of cut, common in homes of the era, produces flooring that is harder and more stable than plain-sawn floorboards—and more beautiful. These floors had yellowed over time and needed refinishing, but the distinctive grain shone through.

This house was a gem, a true estate from a forgotten era. The formal staircase divided the home from left to right and from front to back. The listing photos had given the stairway significant prominence, but something didn't look exactly right. I'd need time to analyze what was going on there.

The servants' staircase in the back of the house was narrow and steep. No modern family would feel comfortable letting their loved ones navigate those stairs—they were too dangerous. That staircase would have to go. Because it wove through all four floors of the house, it would require significant creativity and expense to redesign.

It took us about an hour to finish exploring. We thanked Dustin for his patience and told him we'd get back to him.

DRIPPING WITH POTENTIAL

I now had more questions than answers about this house on Madison, but I recognized a familiar feeling—the excitement of finding a diamond in the rough and the recognition of the enormous challenge it would be to undertake it.

The dangerously narrow servants' stairway would have to go.

"It's a pretty cool house," Dale admitted.

"Totally," I agreed. "The potential is dripping from every room."

"I don't think we should pursue it," he said. "The low purchase price makes it tempting, but the cost to fix it would be multiples of that. Besides, aren't we at an age when people start slowing down? Taking on this project would not exactly be slowing down."

We continued to talk about the house the next day, and I couldn't shake my growing interest in it. I'd always loved a good challenge, and even in disrepair, the Madison possessed an indescribable elegance. I wanted to restore it to its former splendor and usher it into a modern era.

I love the excitement of finding a diamond in the rough.

"I just keep coming back to the potential in this house," I told my husband.

"I know, but think about the immensely complicated remodel," Dale countered, "not to mention the resources it would require."

This is always how it goes with Dale and me. I'm not great at analyzing the downside of things. If I underestimated the financial risk on a house like this, it could be pretty serious. With so many unknowns, the project could easily become the ultimate money pit.

"The materials would be exorbitant," I admitted. "Plus, we'd have to hire a contractor."

We were both doing the numbers in our head. They were big numbers. We sat in silence, stumped.

"Unless . . ." I began. I think I saw Dale cringe. "Unless we took it on with a partner! Remember how we bought that four-flat, the Bvilding, in partnership with our friend from church? What if we did the same thing with this house?

What if I did the design work and we found a partner to do the remodeling work, and we went in fifty-fifty? Cory and his family's company could be perfect. He just told me not two weeks ago that we needed to do another project together."

It sounded brilliant and simple.

Dale and I sat there looking at each other. I knew what I wanted to do. "Go ahead. Call Cory," Dale said. "Let's see what he has to say."

GOOD DESIGN: *Spot Water Damage*

When Dale and I viewed the house on Madison, we spotted several places with water damage. In older homes, damage from cracked foundations, leaky roofs, or broken pipes is common and can cost thousands of dollars to repair.

Over the years of examining older houses, I've learned to check five key things when looking for water damage:

- *Ceilings and walls:* Water that seeps through a leaky roof will sometimes pool above the ceiling or drain down the inside of a wall. Look for brownish rings, bubbled paint, or drip lines in paint or wallpaper.

- *Windowsills, doors, porch floorboards, and rails:* Rain, melted snow, humidity, and condensation on unsealed or cracked windows can cause water damage. Look for doors or sills that are warped and windows that stick. Sitting water leads to wood rot and insect infestation, if not corrected.

- *Mold:* Mold is a major health hazard and must be cleaned and sealed to pass a home inspection. Mold flourishes where it's damp, so check in the attic, in the basement, behind walls, and on flooring for damp areas or any signs of mold. If a basement has flooded previously, it must be treated for sanitation and mold remediation.

- *Foundations and walls of basements and crawl spaces:* A house's foundation can develop cracks from earthquakes or from settling over time. Look for cracks, old repairs, and the smell of dampness or mold in basement-level rooms or spaces.

- *Roofs, chimneys, balconies, and terraces:* Check for missing roof tiles, clogged or missing rain gutters, damaged chimney flashings, and improperly pitched balconies and terraces. If flat spaces aren't angled with a slight pitch away from the home, water can drain inward and cause damage. You'll also want to check for proper drainage around the garage. If a driveway angles downward, rainwater needs to be redirected away from the garage through drainpipes.

If you spot water damage in any of these areas, it's worth your time and money to hire a specialist to accurately determine the cause of the problem and the cost to repair the damage.

GOOD DESIGN: *Give Your Home a Classic Style*

When I began saying yes to whole-house projects like Inverway and Lakeside, I quickly realized there's an art to furnishing a home from top to bottom. While you may never replace all your furniture and decor in one clean stroke, you can still apply principles of good design over time. As you remodel a room, replace old furniture, or add decor to freshen your home, keep these two key concepts in mind:

- *Be flexible.* Choose pieces that could fit into any room. When I furnish my own home, I plan where to put a few large pieces, but the rest could go anywhere. This gives me flexibility to freshen up the home when I get the urge to move things around.

- *Be eclectic.* I'm not a fan of furniture suites or rooms where everything matches. Mix up your wood choices, hardware metals, and lighting styles to create a less trendy, more classic look that will withstand the test of time. A nice mixture of pieces—old and new, fine and rustic—makes a room feel like it was curated over time.

Chapter 15

PARTNERS

When I called Cory to discuss the possibility of a partnership on the house on Madison, he answered on the first ring.

"Remember how you said we needed to do another project together soon?" I asked. "Well, I just looked at a house that you need to see."

"Tell me more," he said.

"It's an old Greek Revival estate home on Madison in Heritage Hill. It has major potential, but it's a beast, and it would take a design–build vested team. I'm thinking you and me. It could be amazing—and once it's done, we can sell it and split the profit."

"What's the address?"

I could hear him clicking keys over the phone. In his classic under-stated way, he replied simply, "I'll check it out."

A few days later, I saw Cory's name on my phone, and I picked up. "Hello!" I said.

"I want it."

That's all he needed to say. He, too, saw the potential of this house.

My heart started pounding. *This may actually happen!*

The next day Cory and I met to discuss how a partnership could work. We discussed a fifty-fifty split, where he'd be responsible for construction management and building materials, and I'd be responsible for design and the finish materials—cabinetry, plumbing fixtures, hardware, lighting, flooring, tile, paint, and decor.

"Works for me," he said. "Lakeside went so well; I say we keep going."

We discussed forming an entity, The Madison Grand Rapids LLC, to make the partnership official. The entity would own the house, and each of us would own the entity, fifty-fifty. Cory would be hired for the build, and I would be hired for the design. We would each pay into the company as money was needed to fund the project.

"I'll have my lawyer set it up," Cory said.

Cory's dad, a real estate broker, handled the negotiations for buying the house. The home had been listed two years earlier for a whopping two million dollars and had been steadily dropping in price ever since. It had just dropped again and was now listed at $775,000 with no potential buyers in sight. We agreed to offer $575,000, and the sellers said yes.

It all happened so fast. I was excited to get into the house and study it so I could learn what it needed and begin planning.

MOVING STAIRCASE AND HIDDEN ROOMS

Once the house closed, Cory began preparing the site. Since we were still forming our plans for the remodel, we didn't want to demolish anything that we might end up wishing we'd kept. He numbered and removed all the doors, then put them in storage. He took out lighting and plumbing fixtures, labeled them, and put them in a portable storage unit on the property. He removed the 1970s-era kitchen cabinetry and laminate countertops.

We hired a draftsperson to measure the entire house and develop as-built drawings so we knew where all the existing walls were. This also gave Cory a pretty good idea of where key structure points might be. We spent a lot of time walking through the house, just trying to wrap our heads around the project.

I imported the as-built drawings into Concepts, the drafting app I use on my iPad. This enabled me to visualize a layer of new walls over the existing walls. I played with different what-if scenarios for getting rid of the servants' staircase and updating the floor plan to suit the needs of a modern family.

In the weeks that followed, I tried many different scenarios, but nothing seemed to work. The biggest challenge was the main staircase, which led from the entry to the second floor. That staircase had been designed to separate the owner and his family in the front of the house from the hired help in the back. It was a focal point, but it created a physical and psychological barrier to the new heart of the home: the kitchen.

> *The kitchen should be a central gathering place, a thing of beauty.*

I didn't want the Madison's kitchen to remain cramped and hidden away in a dark corner. The kitchen should be a central gathering place, easily accessible and inviting.

I wanted the new owners (whoever they might be) to love this space and be proud to share it with guests. I envisioned a beautiful, open room, filled with natural light—a warm and welcoming place.

The flow of the home needed to change as well. I wanted to figure out a way for the entrance to flow toward the kitchen. I considered reworking the path from the front door to the kitchen, but everything I tried ran into structural issues.

"We can't raise that ceiling because the stair landing is right above it," Cory said. Or "No, we can't move that wall because the stairs need that structure to hold them up."

It was always about the stairs.

The final straw came when I realized a king-size bed wouldn't fit up the stairs because the ceiling was too low. In one spot, Cory's head even touched the ceiling of that "grand" staircase. The only way to solve this problem was to tear out the staircase and relocate it.

By moving the staircase from its central position opposite the front door and rebuilding it farther back and to the left, we could create an entry hall and the natural flow of the home would take people straight into the heart of a newly designed kitchen and eating area. *Yes!*

As I studied the plans and walked the house, I noticed that it had been built with great attention to symmetry. The front door was perfectly centered, and the rear window, which I envisioned as the new kitchen window centered above the sink, was in perfect alignment with the front door. The rooms to the right and left of the front entrance were perfectly symmetrical in their width. It was an architectural masterpiece, and I wanted to celebrate it.

I could create an axis running down the center of the house, with the front door and the rear window framed perfectly to show off their symmetry. It would be open and filled with light.

When I updated my sketches with a left-sided staircase and a central hall, I realized I now needed to design something for the right side of that hall. The stairs were four feet wide, which meant I had to create something on the other side of the hall that was also four feet wide.

I started sketching, and eventually I came up with the idea of creating a false wall on the right side of the hallway that would hide two smaller rooms, each four feet wide. One would be a large coat closet and the other a main-floor powder room. As in most older homes, bathrooms and closet space were scarce, so this solved three problems at once.

I designed the wall using jib doors (hidden doors) and paneled them to match the entry's walls. They featured push mechanisms rather than door-knobs, allowing them to blend in with the walls. It was the solution to the symmetry problem. And who doesn't love hidden rooms?

This plan changed everything. If I designed the staircase to reach from basement to attic, it would make the servants' stairways unnecessary. I could lose them and create a truly grand staircase that opened to the whole house.

Changing a staircase is a last resort for a designer, and few contractors relish seeing "move stairs" on their project scope. I would be asking Cory and his team to remove all the stairs in the entire house and then reframe the center of the house to support the structure of new stairs, from basement to attic.

Cory cared just as much as I did about the end product. At the Lakeside remodel, I often heard him say, "I'm not going through all this work to have it be 'almost.' It needs to be done all the way: thoughtful, correct, and with excellent craftsmanship."

I showed him the new plans at the Madison the next day.

"This solves everything," he said. "I hate that we have to do it, but that's our reality. The stairs are out of here. And I like the hidden rooms." *As understated as ever.*

With the front stairs removed and the drywall taken out, we began to see how welcoming this space could be.

He cringed a little as he turned to look at the stairs. "I'll get it done," he said.

And he did.

HISTORIC PRESERVATION

Every step of a major remodel requires permits and approvals from the city. My designs were approved by the City of Grand Rapids building department, but because our structure was in a historic district, any changes to the outside of the building needed approval by the local historic preservation commission—the HPC.

HPC members are often volunteers who sit on a city's board. Their goal is to ensure that irreplaceable historical buildings aren't ruined by the whims of a new homeowner—a mission I support. HPC board members are often knowledgeable about the history of architecture, but they sometimes balk at any change, even if it's executed well and is historically accurate.

I had heard stories from architects and developers about the excruciating level of scrutiny their contractors faced when seeking to make exterior modifications to historic buildings. I didn't have any firsthand knowledge of the Grand Rapids HPC board, but I wasn't looking forward to going through the process.

Thankfully, not many of my desired plans affected the outside of the Madison—no new additions, porches, or doors. The terrace needed repair, but besides tuck-pointing the old brick walls, we weren't looking to change much about the exterior of the house. The one thing that would need approval—and it was essential—was to exchange a skinny set of rear doors for windows.

The doors in question led to the back terrace between the sunrooms. They were located smack in the middle of the home's back wall, where I wanted to position the new kitchen sink. I envisioned large French casement windows above the sink, overlooking the terrace and backyard.

With the sunrooms flanking either side of the kitchen, two doorways already provided access to the terrace. We didn't need a third set of doors, but it would be a tough sell to the HPC because the doors were original to the home. I'd be changing something historic.

I first met with the liaison to the commission to see what I would be up against. "Changing the central doors to casement windows is essential for the kitchen design," I told her.

I worked my hardest on the Madison drawings, which we submitted to the Historic Preservation Committee.

"The commission won't care why you need this change for your interior plans," she said. "They will be concerned about whether the replacement wall and windows you want to build will look original. Put your energy there."

We painstakingly sketched out every detail for another set of windows. We would use this sketch as the template for the replacement windows I wanted to install. We measured and drew every aspect of the windows, with some details drawn to actual size. Then we put together a detailed package of drawings, specs, and information about the materials we'd use. We hoped these plans would cover every contingency when we presented our request to the board.

When we received our meeting date with the HPC, I realized I was scheduled to be at an event in Chicago that day.

"Are you comfortable making the pitch by yourself?" I asked Cory. "We could reschedule."

He sighed. Public speaking wasn't something he would choose to do unless it was absolutely necessary.

"Well, we can't reschedule," he said. "The HPC only meets monthly, and it will delay the project if we put it off till then. I'll present."

"Thank you, Cory," I said, deeply grateful. "I'll pray for you!"

The next night at 7 p.m. I prayed for him. Then I waited.

It was 9:30 p.m. before my cell phone rang.

"Well, that was the most miserable night of my life," Cory said. "They grilled me as if I were some sort of criminal."

My heart sank.

"But . . . they said yes to the windows," he said.

"What? Awesome, Cory! Thank you so much for going through all that. You clearly did a brilliant job."

"Yeah, I was pretty awesome," he said, laughing. I could hear the relief in his voice.

"I don't know why it has to be so hard," I said, "but now we're approved. We aren't asking for anything else. Let's do this!"

GOOD DESIGN: *Get Results with a Historic Preservation Commission*

The local historic preservation commission protects the architectural history of the town. Here are some tips to help you put your best foot forward when presenting to your HPC:

- *Do your research.* Using the ideas in the sidebar "Good Design: Research a House's History" in chapter 4, make sure you know what your house looked like when it was originally constructed—and what materials were used.

- *Design your changes to match the original architecture.* Source original or near-identical materials, and sketch your drawings meticulously.

- *Prepare, prepare, prepare.* Come to your HPC meeting armed with photos, designs, research, and material samples. Create packets and practice your presentation. If possible, ask people who have gotten HPC approval in the past for helpful tips.

- *Only ask for essential changes.* With the Madison, I had several changes I would have loved to make to the house's exterior, but I only asked for the changes we absolutely needed. By minimizing how much you're asking for, you're more likely to get a yes to the changes that matter most.

• *Ask for a do-over.* If the commission rejects your request, ask them if you can incorporate their suggestions and resubmit it.

Remember that you and the HPC share a common goal: to preserve a historic home. Work as a team with your local HPC, and your town, your neighbors, and your home will thank you.

Home is
the nicest
word
there is.

LAURA INGALLS WILDER

Chapter 16

STOFFER HOME

The Madison's challenges were ever-present in my mind, but I couldn't let them consume me. I still had clients to serve and a business that demanded my attention.

When I had posted John and Maura's photos from Inverway and Lakeside on Instagram, more Instagram followers had reached out, wanting us to design their homes. Grace and I booked new projects in Texas, Colorado, California, New Jersey, and New York. This was exciting new territory—but it was just a little scary, too.

TWENTY-THOUSAND-FOOT BRAINSTORM

Grace and I attended High Point Market that April, and on the flight there, she brought up the idea of opening a brick-and-mortar store.

It wasn't the first time she'd made a suggestion like this. With every whole-house project, we struggled to find decor that enhanced the work we'd done to get the house to that point. If we were going to continue doing full-service design, this was a problem we needed to solve.

"If we opened our own shop, we could order decor items for our styling projects that are only available in bulk. We could showcase our custom cabinets, and we'd get wholesale pricing and volume discounts on furniture," she said, her excitement building. "It would be a great way for potential customers to see our aesthetic in person, and they could buy our curated collections of home decor for their own homes. And for you and me, that would mean no more scavenging to style whole-house projects! Plus, how fun would it be to run our own store?"

Opening a store had never been on a list of things I'd like to do, but the more we talked, the more interested I became—and the more it made perfect sense.

We started a list of what we might carry in our store, and by the time our plane landed, we had added a new mission to our High Point trip: find products to carry in our store.

"We're opening a brick-and-mortar store, and we're looking for lines to sell," I told several High Point reps. We were just a little excited.

The more I thought about our current business trajectory, the more I realized this was an excellent next move. It would give us a physical local presence and much-needed office space.

Jean Stoffer Design needed a home. We were a growing staff of five—me, Grace, Katie (my CAD draftsperson), and two new employees: Kelsey (a designer) and Marcey (our operations administrator). Currently, our English cottage was home base. Our staff meetings were held there; product reps, contractors, and clients met us there; and my samples and product books were stashed everywhere—under beds, in closets, and in corners. It was unsustainable.

It made no sense to simply rent office space, because inevitably I'd end up back at my house so clients could see our custom cabinetry and experience the quality in person. At the very least, we needed a display kitchen. And if we needed space for a kitchen, why not also sell products?

On the return flight, I turned to Grace. "As soon as we get home, let's start looking for a place to rent for our store."

WEALTHY STREET

We spent the next Saturday walking around the parts of town we thought would be ideal for a store, and I asked Kelsey and Marcey to research retail-space options in Grand Rapids. Coincidentally, we were having trouble with our internet at the English cottage that day, so Kelsey and Marcey packed up their laptops and drove to their favorite café in town, which happened to be in the liveliest part of Grand Rapids—the Wealthy Street business district in Uptown.

They parked on Wealthy just as a man was hanging a huge "For Lease" sign in the window of a beautiful historic building. They took a picture and texted it to me.

"Where is this located?" I texted back.

"714 South Wealthy Street!"

I love that area! I'd always thought the name of the street was a little odd, but the building looked fantastic. It had two front entrances and an exterior with major potential. Best of all, it was on a main drag, smack in the middle of the most vibrant shopping and restaurant district in the city.

I made an appointment to see the building, and from the minute I walked in, I knew this was our place.

Grace and I were ecstatic. This building would solve a host of problems, plus it would be a fun challenge. Although it felt like the obvious next step for

714 South Wealthy Street— the perfect place for our new store, Stoffer Home.

our business, it would also involve a lot of firsts: my first time working from an office; my first time designing retail space and hiring to have it built out; my first time purchasing inventory; and my first time paying rent.

We signed the lease on Wealthy Street in August, and the next few months were a blur. While I got busy designing the space, we hired Cory and his team to do the build-out, and he secured all the necessary permits.

We had another reason to be excited that fall: our youngest son, Dan, was getting married. He had graduated from Calvin a year earlier and had gotten engaged to a young woman named Marisa, whom we adored. She's a beautiful girl inside and out, and she and Dan are well suited for each other. The wedding was scheduled for October.

We held their rehearsal dinner at 714 South Wealthy Street in the space that—fittingly—would soon be called Stoffer Home. We had so much fun that night. The next day we added our newest family member to the Stoffer clan.

Dan and Marisa's wedding. Our grown kids have brought us more children to love.

Dan and Marisa lived and worked in Grand Rapids for several months before moving to New York City for Marisa's grad school program. Dan had long been interested in the hospitality industry, and when he got a job at the Soho House near Chelsea, he was eager to start learning the business from the inside out.

Dale, meanwhile, was enjoying retirement by being the go-to grandpa and doing repairs at our rental properties. David was still helping us with tenant procurement, and John was busy with commercial photography work but still traveled from Chicago to take photos of our projects. Grace was thriving as my design partner and source of new ideas.

As I reflected on how each of us was now working in some facet of what had once been a tiny business, I marveled at how far we'd come. Each family member was diving deeper into their unique interests in a way that benefited the whole. I couldn't have long-range planned something like this. Who would have guessed that those napping children from two decades ago would one day become full-fledged members of the team?

STORE STOCKING

Opening a store also meant hiring more staff. My operations administrator, Marcey, would manage the store, but I needed a second retail employee. I hired

Paige, a friend of Marisa's, to begin part time in December. She'd be a fantastic addition to the team, managing marketing and promotion for the store.

When it came time to choose inventory to sell, I thought of Grandpa Bradbury. "Only buy fine pieces," he'd told me so often as a child.

"I'd like to fill our store with things of high quality but in a broad range of price points," I announced at our first inventory-brainstorming meeting. "I want every person who comes through our door to be able to afford something beautiful for their home."

Grace and I knew from our home-styling experience what types of products our store's clients would be looking for. We made lists. Kelsey, who had a great eye for the design aesthetic of our company, took our lists to a home decor show in New York City, where she connected with vendors for linens, candles, decor items, and kitchen accessories that were gorgeous and fit our style and price point. We also found a Turkish rug dealer online and bought twenty antique rugs.

"Since we're part of the Grand Rapids community," Grace asked at one brainstorming meeting, "what if we supported local makers, too?" *Great idea!*

We reached out to local artisans and contracted them to create custom products. The lead time was significant, as it would take months to get items designed, created, and delivered. But soon our store would offer pottery, charcuterie boards, custom pillows, and more—all made locally, exclusively for Stoffer Home.

When I designed the shop, I had created space for little vignettes—living room, dining room, kitchen, bath, and bedroom. These "rooms" would convey our style and help customers envision how to use the beautiful products we were offering. The kitchen build-out was primary because it showcased our unique style of kitchen design and our custom cabinetry. Our goal was to not overwhelm people with tons of choices but to have a beautiful collection of items that would all work together.

By Thanksgiving, the Wealthy Street build-out was nearing completion. The construction crew was working hard to get the store ready to hand over to us. We hoped to open in time for the Grand Rapids Shop Hop festival on December 6. This annual event launched Grand Rapids into the holiday shopping season, and half the town would turn out to browse stores in our Uptown neighborhood.

Getting ready to open took longer than we imagined. As we neared the end of November, Grace pulled me aside. "Mom, we can't possibly be ready by Shop Hop," she said. "You need to give it up."

She was right. It was time to back off from my December 6 goal.

"Okay," I said. "Let's call it."

I gathered the team and let them know the Shop Hop pressure was off. "But even if we're not ready to open our doors by then, everyone in town will be walking by the store that night. Let's take advantage of it and give the town a sneak-peek preview."

We had a lot to accomplish before December 6, so the crunch was still on—though with a more realistic timeline.

It was Paige's first week on the team. In the midst of the scramble to put the shop together, she was also trying to learn the inventory system, become an expert on our cabinetry, learn about lighting, and make signage all at once.

"It's a bit like drinking water from a fire hose—in the best way!" she said. She got to know everyone quickly as she jumped in to help.

By December 6, we were semipresentable—with cabinets installed, vignettes assembled, and shelves ready for product. We hung a huge "Opening Soon!" sign in the front window, cranked up some Christmas tunes on our sound system, removed the paper from our windows, and let everyone peek inside as they strolled by.

People couldn't help but stop and look. They watched us stocking shelves, hanging light fixtures, and unpacking beautiful furnishings that would soon be available to adorn their own homes.

I was disappointed that we missed this busy shopping event for our grand opening, but it was still a happy night. While neighboring store owners made lots of sales that evening, we made memories I won't soon forget.

We gave our store the same attention to beauty and function that I would give any client or home. The old building was filled with character, and we let its charm shine through.

There were, of course, plenty of "learn as you go" moments. Case in point: it turns out most shops have rooms in the back for all the extra merchandise that won't fit on store shelves. *Who knew?* We had three rooms in the back of our store. One was a design office, where the whole team could work on projects;

Stoffer Home opened on December 13, 2018.

one was a conference room for meeting with clients, contractors, and product reps; and one was to be my private office. Bye-bye, private office. Hello, inventory room!

Oh, well. I'd rather work in the same room as everyone else anyway.

Besides the vignettes to showcase design and art, the store also included a lighting gallery and tables and shelves to hold product. The sales counter was an antique communion table I'd salvaged from an old church in Chicago.

Our sneak-peek strategy during the Grand Rapids Shop Hop night generated interest from the community. I also did a big lead-up to our grand opening on Instagram. When we opened our doors at 11 a.m. on December 13, folks flooded the store.

Opening-day sales were strong.

"Our total sales were $3,500!" Marcey announced at the end of the day.

Everyone high-fived each other. We were off to a great start.

On day two, our sales were down a bit—$2,200. On day three, we sold $500 in product, and after that, business slowed to a trickle. One day we made only a single sale—a cream and sugar set for $29.

Hmmm.

Then came January and February—and a polar vortex that kept even hardy Michiganders from leaving home unless absolutely necessary.

"The brick-and-mortar store is about a lot of things besides retail sales," Grace consoled me. "It's our office. It's our kitchen showroom. It's our avenue for great products to style our clients' homes. Yes, it's a retail shop, but we aren't dependent on its income to survive."

"True, there's a lot more to it than sales," I agreed. But I kept thinking about it.

We made some adjustments to our inventory. In our early attempt not to overwhelm people with too many options, the store's offerings were a little sparse. We realized people wanted more selection—enough options to have a choice but not so many they felt paralyzed with indecision. We tried to find that sweet spot as we added more inventory to our shelves.

Simultaneously, on Instagram, my followers watched the launch of Stoffer Home with great enthusiasm. But what began as encouragement soon showed hints of frustration. I noticed an increase in comments like "I want to shop in your store, but I live in Texas!" "When will you open a shop here in North Carolina?" and "Where can I find this stuff online?"

I showed Grace the trend.

"We've toyed with the idea of putting the store online," she said. "It's time to get that wheel in motion."

SHOPIFY

Before Stoffer Home opened its doors, we had chosen a point-of-sale system that could manage inventory and track sales at the checkout counter. For those first couple of months, the system worked okay. It had its limitations, but I would give it a solid B for in-store purchases. When we began exploring its capabilities for online sales, we discovered that it was rated poorly for e-commerce.

One day David stopped by the store, as he often did. "I've been looking into online point-of-sale platforms," he said. "We need to switch over to Shopify. Pretty much all successful e-commerce sites use it. It offers everything we need—managing inventory, sales, marketing, analytics, and customer communications—and the integration is seamless."

We had invested money in our current system and spent time uploading all our data into it—including tagging every inventory item in the store with its specific barcode.

"We've got to launch the online store with a platform that will work," David said, "and it has to happen now."

One evening after the shop closed, we all stayed late and made the switch. David printed out strips of price tags with new barcodes, and we wandered the store and inventory room, finding the products they matched and relabeling them. Soon the store was buzzing with energy.

Sometimes the traits that make a child challenging to parent when they're young are the same traits that make you proud when they're grown.

As I pasted new labels onto a row of vases, I smiled. David was at the computer, transferring the last of our files into Shopify. After months of trying to make our old system work, we were finally moving, thanks to his push.

I loved my son's strength and leadership. I thought back to David as a little boy. *All those times when his strong personality had me at wit's end? Totally worth it.* Sometimes the traits that make a child challenging to parent when they're young are the same traits that make you proud when they're grown.

When I hired Paige, her main responsibility had been graphic design and in-store promotion. During the e-commerce platform discussion, she had begun looking at Shopify-compatible website templates for Stoffer Home that might fit our needs and work well with our style. As soon as the decision to convert to Shopify was made, her focus turned to designing Stoffer Home's e-commerce website.

Paige excelled at every task we handed her. She was bright, kind, and hardworking—a natural leader in her own quiet way. When Marcey stepped down as manager, I offered Paige the full-time position, which she accepted.

For the online store, we would start with a moderate selection of products—items that wouldn't break during shipping and would fit into one of the four standard-size shipping boxes we'd bought. Before long, Paige had photographed our online merchandise, weighed each piece for shipping, written product titles and descriptions, and formatted the entire website in a beautiful, welcoming style.

"I think we're ready to launch," Paige told me. "Everything is uploaded, and the site is working beautifully."

So on June 10, at exactly 5:30 p.m., Paige logged on to our website's back end, and she and I pressed the "Go live" button together. We then posted about it on my Instagram account, as well as on the one for Stoffer Home. We watched with excitement and delight when, within the first four minutes, ninety-six people were already shopping at Stoffer Home online. *We did it!*

GOOD DESIGN: *Style a Shelf or Mantel*

Once you've decided which items to display in your home, you'll need to figure out how to arrange them. Here are some guiding principles for putting your favorite things in the best light.

- *Start big.* Begin with a clean slate, then add your largest item first and work your way down to the smallest item.

- *Be odd.* Choose odd numbers of items to display, especially if your space has only a few items. A mantel with three or five items is more aesthetically pleasing than a mantel with two or four items.

- *Vary the size, shape, and height.* Too much of the same thing looks unnatural, so vary the items you're displaying. Too many large items will look uniform; too many small items will result in visual clutter. Put a skinny vase or angular piece next to a round vase. Put a tall candlestick next to a medium statue or a small vase.

- *Mix textures and colors.* Try mixing items made of wood, shiny metal, soft fabric, ceramic, paper (as in books), stone, iron, or natural materials. For example, you could put a brass-framed picture next to a green plant. These pairings create more interest for the eye.

- *Less is more.* Leave some empty space to give your pieces breathing room. If your shelf looks cluttered, remove items until it looks peaceful. Consider rotating items every few months so you get to enjoy the items you removed.

- *Placement matters.* Make sure your decor items aren't lined up in a row like soldiers. Create dimension by placing some pieces in the foreground and others in the background—large or tall ones in the back and short or small ones in the front. Add interest by using risers to elevate statement pieces.

GOOD BUSINESS: *Hire and Fire with Confidence*

Finding great employees takes time and intentionality. I've learned a lot about hiring and letting go of employees over the years. Here are a few lessons I've picked up along the way:

- *Date before you marry.* In the human resources world, short-term contracts and work-for-hire agreements are the equivalent of dating. They allow you to employ someone for a specific, measurable amount of time, during which you can test-drive each other before committing to a permanent position.

- *Don't underestimate people skills.* Observe your short-term hire under a variety of conditions, evaluating them on people skills as well as job skills. Are they a team player? Do they treat others kindly? Do customers and fellow employees like them? Job skills can be trained; a lack of people skills is harder to manage.

- *Create a culture of safety.* When employees have a strong sense of safety at work, they're more likely to turn to you when something isn't going well—and less likely to tolerate bad behavior from one another. It's your responsibility to act when others are being mistreated. Once you spot bad behavior, protect your team.

- *Hire slow; fire fast.* This business adage partners with "date before you marry." Dating via short-term contracts allows you to hire slowly. But if you realize someone isn't working out (and you've spoken to them about the problem, to no avail), let them go. The cost of keeping a toxic person on your team far outweighs the hassle of firing them and retraining someone new.

Chapter 17

JO & JOANNA

With Stoffer Home purring along, thanks to Paige and the team, Grace and I focused on the new whole-home clients we'd signed in various states across the country. In the evenings I worked on designs for the Madison.

MADISON CHALLENGE

It had taken Cory and his crew about eighteen months to complete the demolition, reframing, and replacement of mechanicals (heating, plumbing, and electrical systems) in the Madison. Moving the main staircase alone took weeks of time and effort.

Cory's commitment to quality was evident down to the smallest detail. The house still had all the original doorknobs, solid-brass window handles, hinges, and keyhole covers. These items were irreplaceable, but they had become dingy and corroded over time. Cory removed every piece of hardware and took it home, where his wife, Sarah—and sometimes even their kids—hand-polished each item, restoring them all to their original beauty. *Wow. Above and beyond.*

Because of the explosive growth of both Stoffer Home online and Jean Stoffer Design, our little company had been receiving nationwide exposure. I began reaching out to quality brands that manufactured plumbing and lighting fixtures, hardware, and tile, hoping they would partner with me on the Madison if I photographed and showed their products on my Instagram account. These were brands I believed in—products I'd chosen for countless homes over the years.

In my emails, I highlighted the architectural detailing, noting how beautifully their products could be showcased in such a setting. I sent along photos and design boards to help them envision their products in the Madison's major rooms. And I offered to provide professional images of the completed work, photographed by Stoffer Photography Interiors (John and Maura's business).

They were in.

I began the process of making selections for every finish that would be required in the enormous house, working on one layer at a time. The first layer was plumbing fixtures. I partnered with Kohler and selected fixtures for five full bathrooms, two powder bathrooms, the kitchen, the coffee bar, the butler's pantry, the laundry room, the third-floor kitchenette, and the basement bar. The sheer number of fixtures was so overwhelming that I drove five hours to their factory in Kohler, Wisconsin, to see their products in person and create my extensive spreadsheet.

The next layer was tile and stone. This is a crucial design element in all our projects because flooring and backsplashes must pair perfectly with cabinetry colors while also creating visual variety. I really wanted to get it right. Armed with my list of spaces that needed these materials—basically every room that had plumbing, plus the two sunrooms—I used tile and stone samples to put together combinations I thought would work.

The next layer was lighting. Decorative lighting fixtures are a key part of every project I design. I wanted them all to coordinate but to be distinct, all while providing the correct amount of light for each space. I selected lighting fixtures for every room in the house, plus closets.

Layer by layer, I worked, choosing cabinetry, millwork, countertops, hardware, and paint. It took many months, and I couldn't have done it without my favorite sounding board, Grace.

STOFFER HOME CABINETRY

As more people saw my kitchen designs on Instagram, demand for our services grew. At first, it was exciting. Then it became overwhelming.

Until this point, the only way to get a Jean Stoffer Design kitchen was to hire me. I would meet with the client, interview them extensively to learn about their desires, aspirations, and habits. I would go to their home and measure their space, then meet with them as many times as it took to design their project and select the materials. I then remained available during the construction and installation of every item, down to where every knob or pull should be placed on each cabinet.

Because of the limited number of clients I could serve at one time, only a limited number of people could get a Jean Stoffer Design kitchen. There had to be a way to offer our look to more people, using our cabinetry without the full design I'd been offering for twenty-five years.

One Thursday Grace and I met for lunch with my cabinetmaker, Willard, and his workshop manager. I mentioned how much interest we were seeing in our cabinetry style, and then Grace announced, "We're going to make our cabinetry available online. We just have to work out some details."

I looked at her across the table, my eyes bulging. *What? What was she talking about?* Selling cabinetry online wasn't as simple as opening an e-commerce store with selected, premade products. Every kitchen is unique, which makes kitchen design complicated. It requires knowledge, precision, and problem-solving.

After lunch, I turned to my daughter. "You are crazy—you know that, right?"

"But this idea may be worth exploring," she said, smiling. "We should think about it."

A few days later, I sat down next to Grace at the team design table in the back of Stoffer Home.

"I've been thinking about your idea," I said. "If we designed a cabinetry line with a curated set of options and sizes, we could sell our custom cabinets online."

With my kitchen design clients, we offered full custom cabinetry. Anything I could think of, we could build. But for our online clients, maybe we could design key pieces of cabinetry and make them available in widths of one-inch increments—a big improvement over the three-inch increments of other brands. We could offer our favorite door style and drawer style in a beautiful but limited palette of finishes.

These cabinets would be the core building blocks for a British-inspired, flush-inset, Jean Stoffer Design kitchen. The customer or their contractor would supply all the measurements, and we could hire and train kitchen designers to design these projects from within our line of cabinetry.

"I think it could work!" Grace said.

I explained our idea of developing a curated line of cabinetry for online orders to my draftsperson, Katie, who had already been transferring my hand-sketched kitchen designs into CAD. She knew my style well and had been the lead designer on some of our recent projects.

Katie was all in. "If we can nail this," she said, "it will bring Jean Stoffer Design flush-inset cabinetry into the mainstream market! I've worked for several high-end cabinetry companies in the past, and I know our products are at the top. People who experience our cabinets will be so satisfied. And with expert design included? Wow!"

Katie and I worked together for several weeks, designing a line of cabinets we could sell all over the country.

We knew we needed an online brochure to show customers their options and to coach them on measuring and installation. Katie and I came up with the content, and Paige designed and uploaded a brochure to stofferhome.com. It had all the information customers would need—and it was ninety-eight pages long.

It turns out that most people don't want to read ninety-eight pages to find out about a product. The sheer volume of information was overwhelming.

What they needed was bite-size pieces of information to chew and digest. They needed to ask a question and click on an answer. They needed more pictures and illustrations.

"We need a separate website, just for cabinetry," Grace said.

Paige got busy building another website, stofferhomecabinetry.com, which used an FAQ approach. We tried to write every possible question people might ask and then answer it, short and sweet. We read through each answer over and over, asking ourselves, *Does this make sense? Does it work for someone who isn't a professional kitchen designer?* Then we linked the cabinetry website to stofferhome .com, and for the second time that year, we hit the "Go live" button.

We received many inquiries, but turning those inquirers into customers was a challenge.

"It's a big purchase," Grace said. "Let's be patient. Our target market of design-savvy homeowners can't find our specific look anywhere else in the country, but they'll want to think about a decision like this for months before they purchase."

Time would tell if inquiries would ever become orders.

HOUSE BEAUTIFUL

Decades ago, I had turned down Willard's book of business to design cabinetry for a whole subdivision. Rather than choosing a fast rise in success at the expense of my husband and kids, I'd followed God's prompting and chosen to spend more time with my growing family, not knowing what lay ahead.

For two decades, the business had grown slowly, with one small opportunity at a time—in keeping with whatever season of life I was in. I had no regrets, and I was proud of how far Jean Stoffer Design and Stoffer Home had come. Deep down, every little success still felt like a surprise, and I embraced each one with gratitude.

So when Jo Saltz, editorial director of *House Beautiful* magazine, called about partnering on a project, I was beyond surprised.

"I follow you on Instagram and saw the announcement of your launch of Stoffer Home Cabinetry," she said. "I love your British kitchens and flush-inset cabinets. I'm

I'd followed God's prompting and chosen to spend more time with my growing family, not knowing what lay ahead for my business.

getting ready to remodel my personal kitchen, and we're thinking of doing a series on what goes into such a project. We'd love to use your cabinetry and chronicle the whole design and remodeling process in a YouTube video series and a full spread in the magazine."

What? I couldn't believe my ears. *House Beautiful* is a top-tier design magazine with a huge following on social media. To be featured in *House Beautiful* is a serious compliment, but to be invited to design the kitchen of its editor? I had no words.

Correction: I had three words. "I'd love to!" I told Jo.

I'd been interviewed for magazine articles over the years but had never filmed anything for video. This was new territory—and a fantastic opportunity. It would be a huge boost to raise awareness of the Stoffer Home Cabinetry line. The exposure could feed a business that was now poised to provide our British-inspired kitchen aesthetic to more people than I could have handled myself. Additionally, it was a way to involve more young designers who were interested in working with us.

It was a delight to meet House Beautiful *editor Jo Saltz and discuss renovating her kitchen.*

I flew to New York to meet with Jo and the *House Beautiful* production team. I knew I would love working with Jo when she said, "Everything happens in the kitchen. It's the hub of our entire house." *Yep!*

When I arrived at the Saltz home, I could tell Jo was nervous.

"Save us from ourselves, Jean," she said. "My kitchen is disorganized, messy, and chaotic. It's bursting at the seams. I'm just . . . embarrassed."

"Jo, in no way am I judging you!" I said. "I have been exactly where you are—a mom of young kids who is also running a business. Believe me, my kitchen often looked like this when my kids were little."

"But you're accustomed to seeing such beauty and elegance!" she said.

"Well, if it looked great, there would be no need for me," I said. "And what I see right now is a woman who wants a kitchen that functions better for her family. That, to me, is beautiful."

And with that, Jo relaxed. The production crew followed us through the kitchen as she and her husband, Scott, showed me all its problems. Then they filmed me interviewing them, asking a ton of questions so I could design a kitchen I knew they'd love.

Over the next month, I worked on their project based on their responses to my questions. It was a great chance to showcase the versatility and beauty of Stoffer Home Cabinetry.

When my design presentation was ready, Jo, Scott, and the videographer flew to Grand Rapids. We filmed the presentation in our conference room at Stoffer Home.

I was getting a little better at acting natural while the cameras were running. It was actually starting to be fun. Jo and Scott made their final selections based on the options I presented, and we were off and running.

Grace and I had just completed a whole-house project in Ada, Michigan, and I was pleased with how it turned out. We employed our new line of cabinetry throughout the home. John photographed the project (which we dubbed "Ada Modern Classic"), and Grace suggested camera angles from a comfy chair, her third baby—newborn Jane Elizabeth—in her arms. John's images were stunning, and I wondered if Jo might think *House Beautiful* readers would be interested. I sent her the link to the gallery.

She wrote back immediately. "I think our readers would really want to see this project! Let's run it in the issue right before the issue where I debut my completed kitchen."

In just a few months, John's photos of our Ada project would become a multipage spread in *House Beautiful*, seen by hundreds of thousands of people. The month after that, our cabinetry would be seen again in Jo's own kitchen.

"Your cabinetry line will be getting a lot of exposure soon," John said. "Are you ready?"

I knew I wasn't. But I also knew that the intern I'd hired the summer before, Ella, would graduate from design school soon and would be looking for work. Ella was bright, personable, hard-working, good at CAD, and eager to learn. She would be a great asset in helping us keep up with increased demand.

Ella and I started emailing, and soon it was confirmed: she would begin working as a design assistant at Stoffer Home Cabinetry on June 1.

This is my favorite room in our Ada Modern Classic, featured in House Beautiful.

The kitchen project for the *House Beautiful* YouTube series and magazine spread was coming along nicely. I enjoyed going to New York to film each segment, and I was thrilled with how the kitchen was turning out.

We wrapped up the series by shooting the big reveal in January 2020. The timing would turn out to be fortunate indeed.

MAGNOLIA NETWORK PILOT

Working with Jo and Scott Saltz for *House Beautiful* was the first of two surprising opportunities that came my way around the time we launched stofferhome cabinetry.com. The second started with a voice message from Sarah Kuban, an executive at the Magnolia Network. I returned her call with no small amount of interest.

"I looked you up on Instagram," she told me after a minute or two of friendly chitchat. "But I'd already heard about you from Joanna. Joanna Gaines, that is."

My eyes got big, and I could feel my heart beating out of my chest.

"Your son John has been photographing for the *Magnolia Journal* with Chip and Joanna in Waco, and evidently he and Joanna talked about you. She wants to know if you'd be interested in filming a pilot for their new Magnolia Network."

Wow.

Grace and I had been approached by a handful of other production companies over the past year. They thought a mother-daughter design team could make for interesting television, but those conversations hadn't turned into anything. But Chip and Joanna Gaines? Like half the country, I was a fan of their show, *Fixer Upper*, and I loved how they had fun together. It was a breath of fresh air to watch a television show without manufactured conflict.

I'd heard they were starting their own network, and I liked the type of shows they wanted to create—inspirational, uplifting stories about real people. Sarah had my full attention.

She asked me many questions about our family, the business, and my outlook on interior design. She asked what I was presently involved in—design projects, our store, our grandchildren. She said she'd get back to me if they wanted to pursue the idea further. I thanked her for the opportunity to connect.

On my end, I wanted to talk with my board of directors—and by that, I meant Dale and the kids.

When the whole family was in town the following weekend, I seized the moment to bring it up. Once all the grandkids were fed and in bed (spread all over the house, in closets and every bedroom), we adults sat down for an uninterrupted meal.

I told them about Magnolia and the pilot. Almost everyone thought that doing television would be off brand for me and the company. We were known for classic, timeless style and high-end quality. The kids worried that producers might try to make me look like a freak or drum up *Bachelorette*-style drama just to get good ratings.

I understood their concern. On most shows, it seems like the whole remodeling project is completed in days or weeks. That type of schedule is completely incompatible with the way we do projects. My style is "slow flip," with an emphasis on timeless quality over economy and expediency. My projects take so much more time than I'd ever seen portrayed on TV, and they cost more money.

Besides, I wasn't a cute young designer. I have wrinkles. My style is not "on trend." Would viewers relate to me? Would they like my work?

Then John spoke up.

"Look, it's only one show," he said. "And I promise this won't be trash TV. Magnolia is a class act. If I were you, I'd say yes."

I said yes.

The timeline from saying yes to filming is surprisingly slow, but in November 2019, we began filming the installation of the Madison kitchen for the Magnolia

Filming the Magnolia Network pilot for Point of View.

Network. I was grateful I'd cut my teeth on video production during the filming of the *House Beautiful* YouTube series. It helped me feel more comfortable in front of the camera this time around.

It was interesting to see what it takes to film a show, and the people at Big Table Media (the production company Magnolia hired to film the pilot) were brilliant storytellers and artistic cinematographers, committed to documentary-type reality told in a positive and inspiring way—the polar opposite of some reality TV shows that drum up fake drama.

We finished filming most of the pilot in January 2020, the same time the *House Beautiful* team filmed the reveal for Jo Saltz's kitchen. The Magnolia crew would film the Madison kitchen's reveal as soon as Cory and his crew completed it. But things didn't—and couldn't—go according to plan.

GOOD BUSINESS: *Say Yes to Low-Risk Experiments*

I knew nothing about television production, so by agreeing to shoot one pilot for the *Magnolia Network*, I was saying yes to something outside my comfort zone. But this low-risk experiment was enlightening, and it led to other opportunities. Low-risk experiments can offer huge reward at minimal cost. Look for opportunities that can help you grow—in your business, design, and relationships.

- *Say yes to a new task.* You might love it, or you might not. Either way, you'll learn a new skill and get out of your comfort zone in the process.

- *Volunteer your skills.* Maybe your church, school, or local organization needs a skill or service you can provide. You'll help others—and gain experience in the process.

- *Take a trip with a friend.* Experience a place you've never been before. You'll expand your worldview, make memories, and learn new things in the process.

Chapter 18

SHUTDOWN

For weeks we'd been hearing in the news about something called COVID-19, a highly contagious virus that had begun working its way across the globe. The deadly disease soon caused a worldwide pandemic.

On March 13, 2020, in an attempt to slow the spread of this virus, the governor of Michigan—along with most other governors across the US—shut down the state.

Schools and colleges closed. Theme parks and event venues closed. Hotels, restaurants, and churches shut their doors. Anywhere large crowds gathered was off limits. Only businesses deemed "essential services" could remain open.

The shutdown affected the work of everyone in our family in one way or another. Shooting a reveal for television wasn't deemed essential, so we had to postpone the shoot. Further, construction sites were shut down in Michigan. The Madison sat unfinished, empty. Home-decor stores like Stoffer Home don't offer essential services, so we had to shut our doors.

Dan called from New York. "Mom, Soho House shut down," he said. "I just lost my job, and Marisa's grad school program just announced they are going virtual. We're getting out of New York and heading to Grand Rapids. We can figure things out when we get there."

They arrived in Michigan the next day and moved into a garage apartment at Marisa's parents' house.

John and Maura hunkered down in Chicago. Their photography business had ground to a standstill too, since large gatherings like weddings and small gatherings like commercial photo shoots were canceled.

Just weeks before the shutdown, Grace and Ted had decided to reroute how they did life. Ted had quit his job to focus on finishing and selling their current house and buying a less expensive fixer-upper that he'd work on himself. They would share parenting responsibilities whenever Grace was working on a project with me.

David homeschooled the kids while Kristy, now a CRNA (certified registered nurse anesthetist), was busier than ever at the hospital, working full time and newly pregnant with their third baby.

It was an eerie, unsettling time. It felt like our country was in a free fall. No one knew if this was a short-term catastrophe or the final apocalypse. The stock market lost a third of its value in fifteen days. Warehouses and distribution systems shut down, so store shelves were practically bare. With everyone at home, freeways and sidewalks were empty.

The shutdown had an immediate effect on every aspect of my business. The brick-and-mortar store was shuttered, and even our online store was hit hard. The week after the shutdown, our sales decreased by 99 percent. Buying home decor clearly wasn't high on people's priority lists at a time like this.

The design business was feeling it too. Several design clients pulled out. People put their kitchen cabinetry and furniture purchases on hold.

Our governor announced that only one person at a time could be inside a building that was shut down unless they lived in the same household. Either Paige or I would go to the store from time to time, but other than those trips or other essential tasks, I stayed home.

Thankfully, Dale and I remained healthy, as did our kids and grandkids, and we were still able to get together with them.

Grace and I talked daily over the phone. We had a few out-of-state projects that were still in process, and since they were in different states with different shutdown rules, most continued with their construction. Since Michigan construction sites were shut down, none of our local projects could move forward.

WHAT IF . . . ?

For months I'd been traveling like crazy for projects all over the country. Now everything stopped. It had been years since life was this still and the demands on my time were this minimal.

At first, I wasn't sure what to do with myself. I played the piano and took walks. I continued my morning quiet times with God. Dale and I watched the news. All the while, my mind was whirring. *What in the world is going on? And how long will it go on?*

The government offered financial help to small-business owners, including Paycheck Protection Program (PPP) loans. Business owners who agreed not to lay off any employees during the pandemic could have their loans forgiven. I applied for and received a PPP loan, so I could keep all my employees on full time, but I had to call Ella and postpone her June 1 start date.

Times of crisis can bring out the best in people, and two Instagram influencers, Chris and Julia Marcum (of @chrislovesjulia fame), were a great example of this. They rallied their large Instagram community to help businesses by hosting a small-business promotion weekend. If we sent them our information, Julia would post about the business and drive traffic toward our shop. Most businesses—ours included—planned to offer a 20 percent discount storewide.

We sent our information for Stoffer Home, and Julia posted about us. People jumped in to support us and many other small businesses that weekend. Online sales were strong, and it was a huge shot in the arm.

The prolonged stillness had been good for me, but two weeks into the shutdown, I felt it was time to act. I called for a team meeting via FaceTime.

"What are people feeling right now?" I asked the team. "What could we offer at Stoffer Home to meet people's needs?"

One of our take-care bundles.

We started throwing out ideas.

"Everyone is so isolated, and we can't really reach out to comfort loved ones who are sick or frightened," Paige said. "What if we offered 'take-care bundles' at a discount? For example, we could bundle one of our bars of handmade soap with a linen dish towel. People could send bundles to their loved ones."

Everyone loved the idea, and the whole team started brainstorming different bundles we could create. By the end of the meeting, Paige had several bundles to assemble, photograph, and upload to the website.

When they went up for sale at stofferhome.com, our hunch was confirmed: people wanted to comfort their loved ones, and our bundles helped them do just that. Paige went into Stoffer Home every day to pack and ship the orders.

Grace and I continued to brainstorm. How could we help our business survive a global pandemic? We started to ask each other "what if" questions.

"What if Stoffer Home has to stay shut for a long time? Will our online sales keep us afloat?"

"What if our online store sales really take off? Are we ready for that?"

"What if publicity from the *House Beautiful* series brings a lot of clients to Stoffer Home Cabinetry? Can Katie and I handle all that work by ourselves? Is our cabinetmaker ready to meet increased demand?"

We had another team meeting via FaceTime the following week.

"Sooner or later, people will be itching to get their lives moving forward again," I said. "They're spending all this time at home; maybe they'll want to improve their living spaces. Let's help them shop online by uploading as many products as we can onto stofferhome.com."

Compared to our full inventory in the retail store, our online store stocked mostly small, lightweight, easy-to-ship items. It was time to dramatically increase our online offerings and figure out a way to ship large, heavy, breakable items.

Paige got busy photographing everything in the store, writing descriptions, and posting dozens of new products every day. She fulfilled orders, handled customer service for those orders, ordered more inventory, and received and tagged that inventory. *Whew!* It was a lot.

It wasn't long before Paige's efforts began to pay off with an increase in sales. Perhaps people had been sitting at home long enough to think, *I'm spending every day in this house, and I want to love my space. It's time to do some things to make it nice.* Whatever the reason, Paige was soon spending four or five hours a day packing orders, leaving her little time for marketing, ordering, and website management. She needed help.

Her husband, Patrick, had been furloughed due to the pandemic shutdown. Would he consider coming in to do order fulfillment? Patrick agreed to join the team and immediately made a big impact at Stoffer Home, getting our online orders out the door quicker than ever.

> *We weren't victims, after all. We needed to find smarter ways to thrive.*

After weeks of feeling handcuffed by the shutdown, I loved being back in action mode. Some businesses had been hit in ways they couldn't recover from, and I ached for them. We couldn't change these adverse circumstances, but we didn't need to surrender to them. So we did our best to turn things around in the areas we could control. We weren't victims, after all. We needed to find smarter ways to thrive.

LIFT

Jo Saltz's YouTube series and the two latest issues of *House Beautiful* generated a flood of interest about our online store and Stoffer Home Cabinetry. Inquiries were on the rise.

Our administrator for Jean Stoffer Design had willingly added Stoffer Home Cabinetry inquiries to her responsibilities, but it was a tough job. She had no prior cabinetry experience and was trying to learn while working remotely. It was too much. What I really needed was someone to focus solely on cabinetry.

Near the end of May, Dan learned that the Soho House wouldn't be reopening any time soon and Marisa's master's program wouldn't be going back to in-person classes in the fall. They decided their short-lived time in New York City was over, which was quite a loss of dreams. They left Michigan with an empty truck, drove to New York, packed up their apartment, and drove back to Grand Rapids to begin a new, unknown season of life.

By early June, quarantine restrictions began to lighten, and we were able to open the doors of our store in Grand Rapids for in-person shopping. Online sales at stofferhome.com returned to our pre-COVID numbers, and inquiries about our online cabinetry had risen sharply too. Should some of those inquiries turn into customers, I'd need more design support. It was time to onboard Ella so she'd be trained and ready as a designer. She started on June 15, a mere two weeks later than we'd originally planned.

We still needed an educated salesperson who could dedicate themselves solely to Stoffer Home Cabinetry.

"Dan would be perfect," Grace said. "He's engaging, he loves learning new things, and he's a great communicator."

> *Getting a front-row seat to watch my children flourish as adults has been one of my favorite things about being a parent.*

I loved this idea. I pitched a job description to him, and he was in.

"We want to stay in Grand Rapids," he said. "Marisa can finish grad school online, and I love the job you're describing."

And so Dan, our fourth child, joined the business on July 7, 2020.

As our kids became adults, it was gratifying to see their skills and passions emerge as they took on new responsibilities and became stakeholders in their own lives. Getting a front-row seat to that process has been one of my favorite things about being a parent.

Dan learned on the job, mastering the vocabulary of cabinetry and kitchen design. He became our resident expert on how our cabinetry process worked, including how we move through each design phase and the distinctives that make our cabinetry so special. He was knowledgeable and engaging, which made him a natural at managing inquiries. He also developed a formula to provide clients with ballpark estimates, which brought immediate results. He booked several Stoffer Home Cabinetry jobs, and we were off and running.

NEW NORMAL

The shutdown had significantly hampered our design business, but slowly people began to emerge, like turtles poking their heads out of their shells, making adjustments to a new normal. Video conference calls from home became the new norm for employees everywhere, and suddenly people realized how much time they were spending in their houses. They cared even more about their homes than they had before the pandemic. I sensed tremendous potential.

After seven weeks, the construction shutdown in Michigan was lifted. Cory and his team dove in at the Madison, working to finish the kitchen so the production crew could film the final scenes of our pilot. When the restrictions lightened further in July, we shot the grand reveal.

As I walked the film crew through each detail of the gorgeous space—from the brass inlay in the stone countertop to the coffee bar to the meticulously reproduced windows above the sink—I was proud. And even though the vast majority of the house was still months away from being done, I could see the light at the end of the tunnel. One finished room was the start of something that was going to be profoundly beautiful.

The production company setting up the cameras to film the countertops for the Magnolia Network pilot.

It was always a joyful day when clients who had put the brakes on projects called us back and said, "We're ready! Let's get started." Stoffer Home continued to show steady growth, and cabinetry inquiries began turning into cabinetry customers.

We had survived a global pandemic and were back in business.

⬡ GOOD BUSINESS: *Start Small and Grow Slow*

We survived the pandemic in part because we had a solid foundation. We could regroup, work as a team, and try new things. My business has been thirty-plus years in the making, the product of learning as I go and relying on word of mouth to grow. The advantage of this approach is that our company is made of solid stuff. It's not a house of cards that might crumble if external circumstances change. Here are two advantages to building a business slowly:

- *Less financial risk:* I spent next to nothing on launching my business. This gave Dale and me peace of mind because a business failure wouldn't ruin us financially.

- *Time for skill development:* By starting slowly, I learned my craft at a steady pace. When I made mistakes, they were small enough to absorb, even though they felt significant at the time. I had the bandwidth to come up with a solution to fix them, to learn from them, and not repeat them when the stakes were higher.

*When love
and skill
work together,
expect a
masterpiece.*

JOHN RUSKIN

Chapter 19

SLOW FLIP

Moving the Madison staircase had been extremely challenging for Cory and his crew. The progress was slow, but I'm okay with slow. Quality work takes time.

The sequence of construction called for an elite level of creativity on Cory's part, and he delivered. He led his crew to execute every aspect of my design for the home faithfully and conscientiously. He reconstructed a one-hundred-year-old home and equipped it for its next one hundred years—and beyond.

As wonderful as all this was—a spectacular historic home with beautiful design elements and expert execution—none of this was cheap. It soon became obvious to Cory and me that the "then we'll sell it and split the profit" part of our plan was not going to be possible. There would be no profit on this project. The cost (and time) required to remodel the Madison was well past the break-even point. We might never find

The Madison staircase in its new location, allowing a clear view from the front door to the kitchen in back.

I'm okay with slow. Quality work takes time.

---

a buyer willing to pay what the Madison cost us. Cory and I knew we had to finish the project, but every day of work was putting us further in the hole.

Ever since our financial near-miss with the Edgewood remodel in Chicago, going over budget has freaked me out, so this new reality was upsetting. Dale and I talked constantly about what to do with the Madison, and the topic occupied the conversation of many family dinners. None of us could think of a workable solution.

Then Dale and I went to dinner with two dear friends, Bill and Laurie. I laid out my problem to get their input.

"Back when you embarked on this project, you must have had some ideas about what you wanted to achieve," Bill said. "What were those goals?"

Good question. "Well, when this all started, I was energized by the potential of the home itself," I said. "I imagined it as a slow flip that people could follow via Instagram. I hoped to try new things in design and chronicle how big problems like the staircase get solved. I pictured taking hundreds of "before" and "during" shots, furnishing and decorating the entire house, and photographing with John to capture images of our monumental accomplishment."

"Then I suggest you buy Cory out," Bill said. "Sell your English cottage and make the Madison your home. What better way to showcase your work? It solves every problem you described. Cory understands the financial dynamics. He has been living with them for many months—years, actually. If you buy him out, he's whole financially. Plus, it gives you a chance to keep the house for your business and enjoy it as your home."

What he described sounded like a win for both Cory and me, businesswise. Having access to the home every day could be helpful for many reasons. And the idea of living in the Madison made my heart leap. Throughout the remodel,

Dale and I had slowly fallen in love with the house. Layer by layer, it had begun to feel like home.

Dale and I kept talking long after dinner, and the more we talked, the more we warmed to the idea. We both loved that the Madison was big enough to hold our entire family. Currently whenever we gathered, our English cottage would be bursting at the seams with kids, spouses, and grandchildren. The Madison, by contrast, had room for everyone.

I decided to share the idea with Cory. Early the following week, we met for coffee.

"I think I have a solution to our dilemma over the finances at the Madison," I said. "Let me buy you out."

Cory's eyes grew wide. "What did you just say?"

"I'd rather Dale and I buy the Madison than sell it at a loss."

"How does Dale feel about it?" he asked.

"We've talked about it a lot. He's in full agreement."

"You realize we already have put more into the house than its current market value, right?" he asked. "What's the catch? You and Dale really want to live in a ten-thousand-square-foot house?"

"Not exactly, but I'm looking at this as a business investment more than a real estate investment. It's obviously too much house for us, but I can see us enjoying it with our family and utilizing it for many aspects of the business. If we own the Madison, both you and I would still have access to the house to showcase our work."

"Okay then!" he said. "Why wouldn't I accept that offer?"

"Do you need time to think about it?" I asked.

"I already feel a huge sense of relief, like a huge burden is off my back," Cory replied. "The answer is yes."

We finished our coffee, hugged, then went to our cars.

I couldn't believe it. During the three years I'd been designing the Madison, I'd thought of it as a home for a theoretical future buyer. Now it would be our home. After months of concern, hours of prayer, and dozens of conversations, just like that, the fear of financial loss was resolved. *God, only you could have engineered a plan where such a big problem resolved in a way that left everyone feeling satisfied. Thank you.*

WELCOME HOME

When the Madison project wrapped up the following month, Dale and I purchased Cory's stake and became full owners of the Madison. We sold the English cottage and moved into the most beautiful empty-nest Greek Revival estate in town.

As I unpacked our boxes and settled into our new home, I couldn't help but reflect on how remodeling the Madison held so many parallels to my life. This house had been a slow flip. It couldn't have reached its potential without deconstruction and rebuilding, yet certain things like major bearing walls couldn't be moved. They had to be worked around, which takes time.

> *When we change the things that need changing and work around the things that can't, the result is beautiful.*

How true this has been in my own life, which has been a slow flip of sorts, as well, with deconstruction and rebuilding along the way. I'd had to make adjustments during different seasons—cutting back on new clients to spend more time with our children, shifting the focus of my work from interior decorating to kitchen design, and adding a spouse or child to the business. Some of these adjustments had been the result of "walls" that couldn't (or shouldn't) be moved. When we change the things that need changing and work around the things that can't, the result is beautiful.

On move-in day I walked through the Madison, and so many wonderful memories flooded my mind. Cory and I had partnered together to solve countless complex problems in design and construction, and it ended with us both thankful for the other's contribution. Best of all, the Madison stands ready to host new memories for our big family—Dale, me, our kids, and the next generation of Stoffers.

THE BRADBURY

Dan had been looking for a hands-on project during the COVID shutdown, and when he came across a used commercial espresso machine on Facebook

Front and back entrances of our new home. The Madison is the perfect blend of business and pleasure.

Views from the restored Madison.

Marketplace—a genuine La Marzocco—he bought it. We're a coffee-loving family, so Dan's purchase interested us all.

"Commercial La Marzoccos sell for five figures new," he told me. "It will be my version of a flip project!"

He began tinkering with the machine at the Madison, where he had access to a 220-volt power outlet, water, and a drain. Soon he had it up and running, providing everyone with espresso.

One day as the team sat around the worktable at Stoffer Home, laptops open, he asked, "Wouldn't it be cool if we had an actual café inside the store? It would feel very European and would totally fit the vibe of Stoffer Home. Customers could grab a cup of espresso and then take their time perusing the store. And the aroma of fresh-ground coffee permeating the air—it does something magical."

I loved the idea. *Could it work?* I knew Dan's long-term dream was to own and operate a boutique hotel, but that's a huge undertaking and investment. Could running an espresso café be a first step for him—and simultaneously benefit Stoffer Home?

As I sat there thinking, I clicked open a promotional email from a vendor who imports French antiques. A photo in the email showed a ten-foot-by-ten-foot set of leaded-glass doors and transoms from an old Parisian apartment. They were gorgeous and filled with character.

I clicked through the images, examining all the details. I read the specs to get the exact measurements. My heart started beating faster. I knew exactly what I could do with those pieces.

I flipped my computer around to show everyone at the table: "Look at these doors!" I said. "I think I know how to build a café inside the store!"

"Wow!" Dan said. "They're beautiful!"

"We could put the café in the front left corner of the store and then use these doors to create a wall between the café and Stoffer Home. Customers would feel like they just stepped into a café in New York, or maybe London or Paris."

I could see it all in my mind's eye. With Dan still staring at the screen, I logged into my account and put the antique doors into my shopping cart. I clicked around some more and found an antique French shop counter and added that to the cart.

By this time the whole team was excited. I proceeded to the checkout and clicked, "Complete order."

"We're opening a café!"

Dan's face lit up. "Okay, here we go!" He returned to his laptop to search for information on all things café—a search I soon learned he had been conducting ever since the La Marzocco entered his life. He would continue in sales at Stoffer Home Cabinetry and add a second job: café proprietor.

For my part, I got out my iPad and started drawing the café design that very day. Dan and I worked together in the coming weeks to determine the logistics for the tiny spot we would carve out for our new endeavor.

The natural structure of our circa-1895 building couldn't have been more ideal for adding a little café in the front of the store. The entrance alcove already had two exterior doors: one entry to the left of the store and one to the right. If we built out a café on the left side, people could enter directly from the sidewalk. Once inside, they could access Stoffer Home through a wall constructed from the antique Parisian doors.

The Bradbury on opening day. How I wish Grandpa could see it!

Dan sourced the best coffee beans and tea leaves he could find. He commissioned our Stoffer Home potter to design custom coffee cups. On the operations side, he researched and executed all the health department requirements. Cory's team built the wall that would surround the Parisian doors. Dale and Dan built bistro tables, and we installed beautiful light fixtures. Paige hand-painted the café's new logo in gold paint on the wall above the back bar.

Our family tossed around several different name ideas for the café. In the end, Dan came up with the name we chose. And on January 21, 2021, Daniel opened the doors to our new European café—The Bradbury.

⬡ GOOD DESIGN: *Find and Repurpose Architectural Salvage*

Nothing adds instant character to a home or business like architectural salvage. The Parisian glass doors I found for the Bradbury instantly transformed that space into something distinctive, welcoming, and filled with personality. In the Madison, I repurposed glass storm windows as room dividers, and in countless projects, I've purchased or repurposed old hardware, built-in shelving, fireplace mantels, farm sinks, doors, and windows. Repurposing items can also save significant money. Where can you find architectural salvage? My go-to places include the following:

- *Search engines and map apps:* Open your web browser or the map app on your phone and search for keywords such as *architectural salvage near me, local architectural salvage, secondhand stores, thrift stores, resale shops,* or *ReStore* (the building-materials stores for Habitat for Humanity).

- *OfferUp, Facebook Marketplace, etc.:* Online sites like these have entire sections for building materials and vintage or antique items. Use their search fields to enter what you're looking for (mantel, storm door, sink, siding, etc.).

- *Pre-demolition sales:* At pre-demolition sales, you can find everything from paving stones to fireplace mantels.

- *Estate sales:* Estate sales can be a good source for smaller items such as vintage crockery, doorknobs, tools, furniture, and linens that can be repurposed in your home.

- *Barn sales:* Barn sales can hold a treasure trove of architectural salvage and barnwood, especially for farmhouse or industrial style design.

- *Your house or building:* Are there items in your house that could be used elsewhere? Check the attic, basement, crawl space, and garage for discarded items that could be repurposed.
    - Could old storm windows become room dividers or greenhouse walls?
    - Could old lumber become decorative beams?
    - Could an old sink become the sink in a potter's bench or garden?
    - Could an old counter become a kitchen island or coffee bar?
    - Could an old wooden ladder hold quilts and throws?

Get creative as you look at each item you find. Where might it add character and distinction? The quality of older items often surpasses that of modern manufacturing, and with a little patience and ingenuity, you can find just the right piece for less than you'd pay for new.

Chapter 20

RISE UP

Our Magnolia Network pilot, for the show *Point of View: A Designer Profile*, premiered on January 2, 2021, via Magnolia Network's streaming service, Discovery+. The filmmakers with Big Table Media absolutely rocked it. The pilot was beautifully cinematic, honest, and inspiring. I was floored.

The show got great ratings and reviews, and the people at Magnolia realized viewers were interested in this type of programming—a fact that gave me a boost of confidence. Viewers seemed to like seeing an older, mature woman featured. Maybe design wasn't just about being trendy and hip. Maybe classic hadn't gone out of style.

I was blown away by the flood of direct messages I received on Instagram. Designers—especially women—from all over the country responded positively to our classic, quality design.

"I feel so understood!" one designer wrote. "I'm not crazy for doing the slow, quality work I do!"

"Love your 'slow flip' approach!" another woman said. "Our culture needs more of your do-it-right philosophy."

"I can't stop crying," someone else wrote. "I'm about your age, and I feel so inspired to try this for myself!"

For me, the most meaningful comments came from young designers who said things like, "This is so encouraging! You gave me takeaways about forming a business, developing a design philosophy, and focusing my design aesthetic. It's as if you're mentoring me from afar."

I thought back to my first Sub-Zero and Wolf Kitchen Design Contest win twenty years earlier, when I'd introduced myself to Mick De Giulio. "You've mentored me from afar," I'd told him.

It was humbling to read similar comments from others who were now looking to me in that light. Perhaps television was another platform where I could influence a new generation of designers and pass on the baton of Grandpa Bradbury's wisdom.

MAGNOLIA NETWORK PRESENTS: *THE ESTABLISHED HOME*

Sarah from Magnolia Network called a few days after the pilot launched.

"Congratulations!" she said. "Your pilot is a huge hit."

"Thanks!" I said. "I have truly enjoyed this little experiment, and I've been surprised and encouraged by people's responses."

"And people want more," she said. "Listen, we're launching Magnolia Network later this year, and we're creating a whole lineup of inspiring shows that will focus on 'home and design' and 'food and garden.' Joanna wants you to have your own show that will take viewers behind the scenes on your designs and help them get to know you and the way you've built your family business. She wants her viewers to get more of your seasoned confidence."

I stared at my phone, trying to take it all in.

"She feels your designs are next level—*mind-blowing* was the term she used. Are you up for shooting a six-episode series of your own?"

"Wow!" I said. "I'd be honored to."

After a few more conversations, I signed on for two six-episode seasons, and we started filming season one in January 2021.

One thing that surprised me about shooting for television is how many hours of filming it takes to capture just one hour of usable footage. For the six-week series, which would consist of six one-hour episodes, we shot for sixty days. That's ten days of shooting per one-hour episode!

The good news is that it was fun. I worked with a group of gifted people, largely in my own home, on our interior design projects. As a bonus, my family got to be part of it too. The crew was kind, positive, patient, encouraging, and talented.

I was also grateful the filming didn't require much travel. For the most part we were in homes I was working on in Grand Rapids. The Michigan-based production team would drive over from the eastern part of the state, spend a day or two filming different aspects of the projects I was working on, and then go home and start planning the next filming. Meanwhile, a postproduction crew in California edited what we shot.

The production team and director shared my passion for older homes whose heyday had come and gone and were now sitting neglected. They focused on six old-house projects, including the porch on the north side of the Madison, the one room I'd left completely untouched during our big project.

I loved the mystery involved in remodeling those homes to their former glory and updating them for a new era. You never knew what you'd find as crews dug into walls to replace outdated systems.

Every house has a story to tell, and our film crew joined me in telling some of those stories. Inevitably a remodel brings challenge, whether it's a post that can't be moved or a beam that cuts into the kitchen but is essential because it supports the roof. I look at these challenges as guardrails. I can't go beyond them or change them, so I need to get creative. I need to find a way to keep that guardrail in place while maximizing the home's beauty and function.

We all have guardrails we can't change in our lives, whether it's past tragedies, emotional scars, or current circumstances. Do we complain about these guardrails and wish they weren't there? Do we just grind against them? Or do we choose to accept that they're part of our story and incorporate them into our lives?

The challenge is to create beauty and function in our lives within the boundaries of our guardrails.

It took us ten months to film the six-week series, which would be called *The Established Home*. We began in January 2021 and wrapped in November 2021. The production schedule was complicated, and I marvel at the organizational skill it took to conceptualize, plan, and film each episode.

It was an honor to be part of a project of this caliber, and we Stoffers were eager to see how it would turn out. The show was set to premiere on the Magnolia Network on New Year's Eve, so we'd have to wait another six weeks before it came out. Throughout that time, I prayed that the finished product would reach a new generation of designers, homeowners, family businesses, and women—especially mothers—who might be inspired to create things of lasting beauty in their careers and in their homes.

> *The challenge is to create beauty and function in our lives within the boundaries of our guardrails.*

MAGNOLIA HOME PREMIERE

I awoke at 5:15 a.m. on December 31, the day our show would launch. Immediately my mind filled with myriad details that needed attention before guests began arriving for the New Year's Eve party/television premiere of *The Established Home*.

Then it hit me: our show was probably live right now! I grabbed my phone from my nightstand and pulled up the Magnolia app. Sure enough, *The Established Home* episodes 1 and 2 popped up as ready for viewing.

I elbowed my drowsy husband. "Dale! The show is uploaded! It's right here!" I pushed my phone in front of his face.

"Let's watch it!" he said, perking up.

"But should we wait? The premiere isn't until tonight . . ."

"We'll call it a sneak preview."

"I'm in!"

We propped ourselves up with pillows. Then I hit play, and we watched our family's story unfold on the screen of my phone. We were mesmerized by the skill of the Big Table Media production team and the way they'd shot and edited the footage. The episodes felt true to life.

Seeing our story told onscreen was a fascinating experience. I was excited, to be sure, but I also felt humbled by all the little backstories that had led up to this season of my life—the many times I'd wrestled over decisions, made mistakes, or struggled with people I hold dear. I recalled times I'd been hurt—or worse, times I'd hurt others—by sharp or unfiltered words. Through it all, we'd built something I'm proud of—not just the business, but a family that works well together professionally and still enjoys each other's company.

How many times had God guided situations in my life? How often had he mitigated mistakes I'd made, circumvented parenting failures, or blessed my feeble attempts to be faithful? With my phone's tiny screen illuminating the darkness, I felt God's grace wash over me—and our family.

What struck me most wasn't the design aspects of the show, it was the interactions with my kids. I couldn't help but notice how far we'd come as a team, and I was one proud mother.

I will never regret the career opportunities I turned down when the kids were young. Investing in my family back then—not just focusing on their academic or athletic accomplishments, but investing in their souls, skills, and interests as human beings—had led to such fulfillment. As Dale and I watched pieces of our story unfold, I thanked God to be receiving such dividends on investments made long ago.

As soon as the credits rolled on episode two, I tossed back the covers, headed to the kitchen to start the coffee, and dove into the day. My friend Rosa, who was a professional caterer before she came to work for us at Stoffer Home, had most of the details for the party under control.

"Let me just run with this," she'd told me a couple of months ago when I asked her to help me plan the event. "This kind of party is right in my wheelhouse."

That afternoon Rosa took command of the Madison, placing a carving station for beef tenderloin at one end of the kitchen island, wine and beverages at the other, and side dishes, salads, and breads displayed artfully in between.

She'd ordered a gorgeous cake, and she and her husband had strung twinkle lights everywhere. The place looked and smelled magical.

A swarm of Stoffer grandkids arrived early with their parents and were swiftly tucked into their beds upstairs. At eight o'clock, the doorbell rang with our first guests, and the grownup time began.

As the Madison filled with beloved friends and family, I was thrilled to see how well the space we'd designed absorbed the crowd. Many guests hadn't been to the Madison yet, and the hidden powder room and coat closet in the hallway were favorites, along with the sunroom, which—even in a Michigan December—was warm and welcoming.

This is exactly how I envisioned this space, I thought. My heart practically glowed.

At nine o'clock, I made an announcement: "Hey friends, thanks for being here! The viewing will start in half an hour, so load up your plates, fill your glasses, and find a seat in the family room downstairs!"

While everyone made their way to the kitchen for refills, I headed downstairs to cue the show on our TV screen. When I clicked on the Magnolia Network, I saw that *The Established Home* was the first show featured. I scrolled down, and under "Trending," our show was number one! *Woohoo!*

One by one, people made their way to the family room. At 9:30, Dale dimmed the lights, and I hit play. As each scene unfolded, I listened to people's reactions. I took their oohs and occasional laughter as encouraging signs.

When the credits rolled, Dale turned on the lights. Looking at each face in the room, I was struck by the power of this moment. I was filled with gratitude for these people—my husband, our kids, and these dear friends, clients, and coworkers who had come to celebrate this event with us.

I rose and stepped in front of the TV. "Friends, I am not exaggerating when I say we would not be here watching this show without each of you. Every person in this room has played a part, either as clients who have entrusted us with your homes or as coworkers who have given your very best to every project we've tackled together or as family members who have learned the art of working together professionally while still loving each other.

"This is the power of community. We are here for each other. We need each other, and when times are hard or things don't go as planned, we have each other's backs. When we allow people to see us for who we really are—not the Pinterest version, but the version with wrinkles and challenges—we discover we're not alone." One by one, I thanked each person for their unique contributions.

It was long after midnight before the last guest headed for home. As I climbed the staircase for bed, I thought with fondness of how those very stairs had given Cory and me fits as we struggled to create a natural flow in the home. Tonight's gathering had proven it was worth the effort.

By the time I slipped beneath the covers, Dale was asleep. I laid my head on the pillow, but my mind was still whirring. I was blown away by the day—and, to be honest, by so many things in my life. I felt an overwhelming sense of gratitude to God, who has brought me so much joy, wholeness, and fulfillment. I am simply a designer who remodels houses, which are nothing more than containers for the humans who live there. I do my best to create designs that help those houses become homes, but design has never been the main thing for me. The main thing has always been the people.

Building a business has given me opportunities and brought me many dear friends over the years, but nothing compares to the gift of family. Having my life so intertwined with the lives of my grown kids feels like an unwarranted treasure from God, and I count myself rich every day on account of the friends and family God has placed in my life.

As I closed my eyes, I thought back to the first time our family gathered at the Madison, for my birthday party the previous August. Our grandkids had lined up along the patio steps to sing my favorite hymn.

The final line of that hymn has become a crescendo for me:

And give him the glory; great things he has done.

I still have far to go in this life. I have much to learn, and I hope I'll never stop growing and becoming the person God dreamed me to be. No doubt there will be new challenges to tackle and new joys to embrace. But no matter what the future holds, I'll give God the glory, each step of the way.

◊ GOOD LIVING: *Help Your Child Rise Up*

I count it a joyful, unexpected surprise that my adult children are also my professional colleagues. Whether or not you own a business that could employ a teen or young adult (and whether or not working with your kids would be a good fit for your family), you can make a difference in the life of an emerging adult. Take note of these areas where you can nurture a young adult in your life.

- *Natural aptitude:* Our son John had a natural gift for taking photos. This turned out to be a huge benefit to my fledgling business. What skills and abilities stand out in the emerging adult in your life? How might these skills be used in a future job or in your business?

- *Relational wiring:* Dave's leadership ability and self-confidence enabled him to jump into our rental-home projects with little experience, and he now serves as general contractor for our slow-flip remodeling projects. Dan's people-oriented style makes him fantastic at managing sales for Stoffer Home Cabinetry and running the café. How is the young adult in your life wired relationally? Where might they thrive in a work environment or your business as a result?

- *Interests and passions:* Grace showed an interest in partnering with me in whole-house projects, and she is passionate about design and style. John's passion for photography and Dan's passion for hospitality shone in their respective roles in our company. What passion or interest could you foster in your child as they grow? How might you encourage and equip a young adult so their passion translates into a future role, whether that's in your company or in another job?

If you can create an environment where you, your family, and your business thrive together, pursue it! Working alongside my adult children in our family business has been one of the greatest joys of my life, and I wish the same for you.

Acknowledgments

Thank you to Jan Long Harris, executive publisher at Tyndale, who originally conceived of this book and ushered it through to completion over a three-year period. Her first call ("I think there may be a story we should share") was filled with hope and expectation. Her most recent call ("I love it") was filled with blessing and encouragement. Thank you, Jan, for your confidence and care.

Thank you to Stephanie Rische and Debbie King, editors at Tyndale, who carefully looked at every paragraph, phrase, word, and punctuation mark, making sure it contributed to the story, made sense, had the right tone, and was grammatically correct, all with grace and kindness.

Thank you to Libby Dykstra, designer at Tyndale, who took the words and images and designed this beautiful book you are holding. I am full of respect and admiration for each step required to craft such an elegant piece. I never knew all the elements involved, and you are good at them all.

Thank you to September Vaudrey, who listened to my story, cared deeply about conveying it thoughtfully; set up a framework for how it should be told; and wrote, rewrote, and counseled me on how to say what was in my heart. It was delightful getting to know a real author.

Thank you to Joanna Gaines, who believed the world was ready for a TV show that featured a woman not exactly in her perky prime.

You believed that watching beautiful design and a happy family would actually be time well spent. I appreciate the investment you made to tell our story in a beautifully cinematic way. And thank you for your vote of confidence and your endorsement of this book.

Thank you to John Stoffer, professional photographer and my dear son. It's true—a picture is worth a thousand words. In your case, they are all beautiful words, as your work evokes a beautiful emotional response. Thank you for your contribution to this book, yes, but thank you also for portraying our design work in such an evocative way over the years.

Thank you to all the friends, family, and others who read various versions of the manuscript and thoughtfully gave your responses, suggestions, and even harsh critiques that made the book so much better.

Thank you, Dale—I'm pretty convinced (well, actually, it's confirmed) that most of what's chronicled in this book would not have happened if it weren't for you. You love me in a way that is selfless yet won't let me get away with anything I shouldn't. I love our morning coffee together. Thank you for everything you've done and still do for me and the family, much of which goes unnoticed but is crucial. I was initially attracted to you for your sense of humor, and I continue to be thankful for it, as it is still the thing that makes me laugh most (accompanied by an eye roll a fair amount of the time). I love those things about you, but mostly, I just love you.

Thank you, Jill Dailey Smith—our multidecade friendship has enriched my life so much. I wouldn't have had half the experiences I've had without you, because you are my "instigator in chief." Thank you for broadening my perspective on life.

Thank you to Laurie and Bill Hamen, who were some of the first to catch on to what might be in store and have prayed for me and counseled me in the most effective and considerate ways. When you have friends who hold the same things dear, they are trustworthy counselors. You, my friends, are that. Thank you.

Thank you, Rosa VanderKolk, my tiny Italian dynamo friend. Our morning walks and on-the-fly prayers and your cooking and straight talk have been God's gift to me here in Grand Rapids. To embrace a new friend at our age is remarkable, and I'm so thankful for you.

Thank you to my parents, Don and Gail Tittle; my siblings, Ann, Karen, and John; and their spouses, Jay, Kurt, and Sarah. We are all the products of nature and nurture, and I think I hit the jackpot with all of you. As Dale says when he's complimented on something, "I chose my parents well." Me, too. In fact, I chose my siblings well, too. I also chose their spouses well. I learned from all of you what it looks like to love the Lord and live according to his purpose. That is a gift that is not lost on me. I thank you, and I thank God for you.

Thank you to my kids, David, John, Grace, and Daniel, and your spouses, Kristy, Maura, Ted, and Marisa. I learned (and am learning) how to pray and trust the Lord because of you. I have experienced deeper joy than I could have imagined because of you. I am inspired by you and held accountable by you, and I feel great love from you. I didn't get to choose what any of you would be like, but I deeply respect and love each of you individually for who you are. I thank God for you every day, and I love each of you with my whole heart.

Thank you to my grandkids, Clark, Frances, Theo, Charles, Brooks, Wes, Jane, Hugo, Gloria, Tommy, and those yet to be born. You are helping your parents seek God while adding untold joy to all our lives. I love you!

Thank you, dear reader, for investing your time to read this story. I pray that it inspires you, no matter what stage of life you're in, to say yes to the Lord and the opportunities he gives and to say no to the things that might cause you to veer from the path. Both are equally important.

Lastly, thank you, God, for your forgiveness, kindness, provision, and faithfulness, and for the trials you allow and the wisdom you freely give. You are truly great and truly good and, as such, worthy of all my praise.

About the Authors

Jean Stoffer is an interior designer who specializes in kitchens, the heart of the home. She and her husband, Dale, have four adult children, their spouses, and a number of grandchildren. Her classic interior design became nationally known through social media. Her design and the envelopment of her adult children in the business is chronicled in her television show *The Established Home* on Magnolia Network. She enjoys encouraging women to love their children and to cultivate their personal and spiritual growth into adulthood and beyond.

September Vaudrey is an author, a collaborator, and a ghostwriter who finds joy in helping people share their stories and ideas with the world. When September's not nerding out on a writing project, she can be found tending her chickens, working in her garden, or spending time with friends and family. She and husband, Scott, live in California near their grown children and grandchildren. Learn more at septembervaudrey.com.

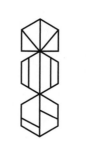